Praise for

GODSPEED

**Longlisted for the 2019 PEN/ESPN Award
for Literary Sports Writing**

"Raw and poetic . . . lean and ferocious."

—The New York Times

"A coming-of-age drama captured through poetic prose and convincing honesty."

—Kirkus Reviews

"A poetically written account by a resilient rebel who skillfully captures what it is like to feel the world through her skin."

—Booklist

"[A memoir] with so much power . . . inspiring."

—Vanity Fair

"*Godspeed* is a memoir for our times—an urgent, hypnotizing account of growing up and growing into one's skin under extreme circumstances. As brutal and original a telling as I can remember—of loneliness, of coping until the center cannot hold. There is darkness here, but in Casey Legler's deft hands it serves the light. A cut-to-the-bone blues song in chapter form, these pages are touched, as she is, with lightning."

—Michael Stipe

"Reading *Godspeed* is an experience as invigorating, beautiful, and punishing as standing under a waterfall. Legler is an unflinching chronicler of light and darkness, loneliness and embodiment, and the deep enchantments of sensation."
—Helen Macdonald, author of *H Is For Hawk*

"Exceptionally talented, reckless, separated from a true sense of herself, Legler could so easily have not survived her early life. The tension here is in how close she comes—by choice, or by default, in settings both elegant and ruined—and is still able to restore herself, her soul, and renew language itself to tell of it. Many of us would be well served by reading the last sentence of this memoir every day."
—Amy Hempel

GODSPEED

GODSPEED

a memoir

CASEY LEGLER

ATRIA PAPERBACK

New York   London   Toronto   Sydney   New Delhi

ATRIA
PAPERBACK

An Imprint of Simon & Schuster, Inc.
1230 Avenue of the Americas
New York, NY 10020

First Atria Paperbacks hardcover edition October 2019

ATRIA PAPERBACK and colophon are trademarks of Simon & Schuster, Inc.

For information about special discounts for bulk purchases, please contact Simon & Schuster Special Sales at 1-866-506-1949 or business@simonandschuster.com.

The Simon & Schuster Speakers Bureau can bring authors to your live event. For more information, or to book an event, contact the Simon & Schuster Speakers Bureau at 1-866-248-3049 or visit our website at www.simonspeakers.com.

Interior design by Amy Trombat

Manufactured in the United States of America

10 9 8 7 6 5 4 3 2 1

Library of Congress Cataloging-in-Publication Data has been applied for.

ISBN 978-1-5011-3575-0
ISBN 978-1-5011-3576-7 (pbk)
ISBN 978-1-5011-3577-4 (ebook)

For all the young ones struck with lightning.
For their friends and for the families.

Author's Note: A Small History in Autism Spectrum Disorder

"When you die, Casey, and they open your brain, that's when they'll see that it's not built like the rest of ours." That's what my lawyer was saying to me as I sat across from him in his corner office in a building on the Avenue of the Americas, topmost floor. I had gotten arrested a few nights before, following a failed attempt to put up a large art installation on my favorite empty lot on East Thirteenth Street—a story for another book. I understand now that he didn't mean this based on my eccentricities but maybe because of something else he picked up on.

When I wrote this book, I wrote it as my story of girlhood, growing up across cultures and languages, a story of resilience in the midst of the unusual circumstances that came along with being a young professional athlete and young addict. Somewhere between the final draft and the book you have now, I was diagnosed with autism spectrum disorder (formerly known as Asperger's—also now known fondly in our family as Aspie).

So—along with the drugs, the Olympics, the abuse, the general disregard for authority or other people, and the ways I coped with my struggled youth—I also inadvertently wrote the story of a young girl child who was on the spectrum.

My hope in disclosing this last bit is that this memoir remain for all the young ones touched with lightning, and that it also bring comfort, understanding, and companionship to those who love them while they find their way.

Yours in friendship,
Casey

Genesis

Winter 1991
Stockholm, Sweden

MY EYEBALLS WAKE UP SIGHING. I'm in bed and don't move. One blink—fourteen—*I'm fourteen,* I say to no one. Light filters through every small square weave of the thick industrial orange hotel curtains. I turn my head away from them and stare at the ceiling. I'm stuck on another team trip. It's 7:00 a.m. The only alarm clock in the hotel is the television, set to MTV, and the music that woke us, and that's playing right now, sucks. My roommate gets up to brush her teeth, and I hear her pajamas walk into the bathroom. I hate her. I look back to the window.

The music changes, and I lift my head from its pillow and stare at the screen. Without taking my eyes off the TV, I reach for the remote next to my bed and turn up the volume.

I can hear my teammates down the hall doing the same. They're opening their hotel room doors to let the sound out, and I hear it seep into the hallway carpet and now my whole body sits up and I watch it: anarchic cheerleaders slowly moving back and forth like they're underwater, arching their backs in a slow-motion dirty school gym, their hair waving rhythm from their long necks down to their tight waists; the boys in loose jeans, t-shirts, and sneakers, on bleachers and head-banging a slow moving mosh pit; and those four notes I've never heard before are playing over and over and over again. I'm seeing my people. I'm seeing home. Nirvana.

My brain clicks. My eyes tunnel to the gym in front of me and I hear it from far away, background noises to my sentences: I have to swim today; I'm at a swim meet; I am wearing sweatpants. Through the sound I look down at my arms and I can't believe they are mine—fast and quick. I flex a muscle in my forearm without thinking and stare at it, flexing and unflexing. I have to wait until tonight to smoke. I have to wait until tonight to drink. "Teen Spirit" lands on all of me, and the cheerleaders arch their backs and show off their tight tits, and my back slouches toward them, hungry from under its t-shirt. My arm drops to its side and my body howls music arms tits on a television and I have to stand it while it does. Blink. I look back up to the screen and what I want is to make the fact that I'm not them go away. I want to be in Their somewhere, not mine, like Them, head-banging away the hollow from the inside.

Stockholm clicks back into focus. Silence. I turn my head and stare with disgust at my roommate, who's just come out of the bathroom. She has a toothbrush in her mouth and white toothpaste on her lips. She is staring at the television too.

Fall 1989
Mont Robert, France

WE HAD MOVED BACK TO FRANCE TWO YEARS AGO into one of the two big white houses on Mont Robert in late summer. The sun would set soft gold over our house, the vineyards behind it and down into the hills, becoming a haze. Our house smelled of clean and freshly painted walls and the long windows full of sky opened out to the gravel driveway. The hill behind it would cool my heated insides and dry a god on my lungs: calm me. The air high into the house ceilings reminded me of going to church in Louisiana, where we had just come from, and the wind came more easily for my lungs when I breathed and looked up. In that wideness there, emptiness would heave cliffs from far away in my body and make it heavy.

I got very sick that year. Too sick to go to the doctor so he had come to us and like kings and queens and pearls on earlobes, his leather satchel walked into my large wide room and leaned over me. I sat up when he did and looked over at my younger sister Sue on her bed and told her that the rocket ship to the moon was ready for our trip. The walls looked red and yellow again and white light was coming through the long windows.

The bigger house on the domaine belonged to a family who wore pearls around their necks and their daughter wore navy sweater vests and white blouses buttoned all the way up to her throat. Off the side of the kitchen, she had a maze made of shrubs higher than my head. The month before school had started, Sue and I had been invited over for tea. We'd sat in large tall chairs with straight backs in a large burgundy living room and afterward, standing erect like ladies at Versailles, had walked through the shrubbery maze. I didn't go back but once after that, when it was really cold and no one was out and no one could see me, lonely in the green walls with the sky as my ceiling trying to stop hearing everything.

We didn't see Dad anymore that year but heard him coming home late at night and, sometimes, his car leaving early in the morning, the wheels making crunch on the gravel drive. The air grew thick in our house: I could slice through it sometimes, making a thin space through which I could just squeeze. More often it just lay on me like an opposite magnet, raising the flesh off my bones—making space that shouldn't be there, and now that I was floating, my skin widened off its body like that—it was even harder to breathe through the rushing sound in my ears.

Mom spent her time crying, tears caught in the eyes that she wiped away when we walked into the new small white kitchen. We knew to pretend it wasn't happening. Sometimes when another stranger-wife would come over, the wife of one of Dad's partners, we were made to go out for a walk with the new children and we would, awkwardly keeping quiet from each other from opposite sides of the road. Ahead of us, strolling wide-hipped next to each other, the mothers would joke that they were going to put widow's walks on top of all their houses: the better to wave good-bye to their husbands who were always gone. Once, with the other kids farther behind us, I asked them what they meant and Mom and the stranger woman bitter laughed and didn't answer. The gravel would crunch the truth under my feet, the linden trees on the path would flit their last leaves before fall and would wave underwater from their branches as we walked by, and everyone would pretend that nothing was happening. I didn't understand anymore why she didn't just leave him, since everything seemed worse for her. I breathed in the sharp fall air full of questions.

Some afternoons, Mom would wait for Dad to come home because it was Sunday and when he did he never brought flowers and my older sister, Polly, and I would pretend we weren't sitting next to each other on the couch in front of the TV and, through the thick white wall in the dining room, hear Mom walk up the stairs to their room and Dad not follow. I'd look down at my hands and the couch would give under me and the lining of the seat cover would become a microscope and I could see the fuzz of each fiber until the light snapped me back and I could hear the high-pitched voice of a song by Mylène Farmer and I could see flickering bright and loud in my eyes the bass screen thumping of another song pump up the jam pump it up while the beat is thumping pump pump and I didn't understand why she didn't just get them herself if she liked flowers so much, and my insides would drop out from under me in a gasp chased by the neon television.

Winter 1991
Stockholm, Sweden

SO THAT MORNING, TWO YEARS LATER IN STOCKHOLM, a fast swimmer now, I walk onto the pool deck and look around for the kids from Brest, Brittany. Cult-like and quiet, I'd been watching them not talk to anyone for the past few days. Hooded and huddled under oversized parkas this morning they walked by me slowly, casting long shadows behind them. When they passed by, the air emptied out from under them. My eyes stared from the shadowed edge of my own parka: *Look at me*. When they finally do, they do it as a team. They stand in front of me—a pack of tall hooded bodies asking me questions that each of them listens to with their heads down and nods for. I feel special and feral—we smell each other. The girls, like the boys, are ugly and fast, like me. They're ghost swimmers, broken and weird, accidental athletes, fallen to the water somehow—maybe because they, too, were born by the sea. Their eyes inset deep in their faces, our bodies carry the knowing of not wanting to be here and the emptiness of loss. It's a low long growl from under our breaths and we hear it. They are the only ones who care, the only ones who understand that this, this is Purgatory and that here we are the no one swimmers and we mean nothing.

I was born three times.

Family legend has it that my sister Polly pushed me into the Mediterranean Sea when I was three. I like the idea of this: two small creatures, sitting on a dock in a quiet port in the gold haze that's the light of the South of France, staring down at the glisten of the water at their feet making shadow patterns on their skin, the light flitting up their calves. Then, curiosity strikes: the bigger one looks over at the smaller one, crouched on her heels, staring at the sparkle shimmers in the water—and pushes.

I was ripped out from under the black, wet glass and wrapped naked in a towel in front of a neighbor stranger. I wondered why his arms were not my mom's and my head echoed rivers of glitter veins and heard nothing. The sharp ice wind I breathed into my lungs split open into a canyon and there was sound there. Each inhale sent shards tearing through it.

That night in Stockholm after the meet, packed into a hotel room of cornered vodka bottles, I get drunk with the Brittany swimmers and they drink like me: hungry. We all get wasted, crawling over each other our drunk and slow-moving limbs sprawling vertigo—larvae on a bed, all of us too crowded, our heads hang off the edge of it. Someone takes a picture of me waving at the camera while I pee. You can't see my face I'm so folded up into it, my shoulders drunk up to my ears. I'm wearing an ugly green shirt with the Olympic rings on it and it's rough against my skin and uncomfortable on my neck. I drink some more and my body flashes lightning and I don't feel my shirt anymore.

Everyone's passed out somewhere on the bed, or slowly crawling, comatose, across the floor. One lightbulb from the bathroom neons over the room, and out of the mounds of barely moving skin, one of the biggest Brest swimmers, Duval, with his broken face, pain rugged eyes, and a chest that pokes out like a bird's collarbone, shoves me up against a wall and muffled here, strangles my throat to kiss me. I gasp and blink away the ceiling and the slow-moving couples in the corners. I try to pull my head away but his big hands keep my face there and his body presses hard up against mine, hurting. The wall makes a sharp edge on my spine. I can't move. And I like it. I fall into him and beg him, a whisper, and he matches my insides to my outsides with his body and I become this deadening place where nothing grows and I don't remember.

At the end of the night, I'm the last one standing. Again. None of it feels better. I've left the dark bedroom and I'm in the hotel lobby with its crushed red velvet wallpaper. I run my hands over it while the receptionist looks at me from behind her desk, and I listen to the lightbulb in the stairwell glow yellow on the burgundy shag carpet. I think I might be lonely, but I shrug my shoulders and hear my thoughts figuring out if I had fun tonight or not and I wander to my room and I look out the window. The sky is turning morning black outside. I pack my bags. We leave that morning, early and without sleep, for our flight back to France. On the plane, I throw up all of my insides: a clear Technicolor green.

That afternoon I get home to a Sunday house—the wooden beams hang limp over the quiet living room. Dad is surely at work—I don't know where everyone else is. I drop my bags in the doorway and stand there listening. I walk to the kitchen and one of the cats pads over and drinks water from the Tupperware at my feet. I watch her fur dapple like she's underwater in the sunshine. The cool edge of the cabinet I'm leaning against reminds me that I'm nowhere and I bend down to grab muesli out of it, shoving the cat out of the way, leaning back up, pour some into a bowl. I hear it clink as the flakes fall into it. I put the box down on the kitchen counter and stare at the perfect Provençal blue-and-white tiles underneath it. They're clean and white. I open the refrigerator—its light wides out. I grab some milk and pour it into my bowl. Through the green spider plants on the kitchen's windowsill, the sun shines a bright afternoon only on my back.

I stand there for a while, in and out of the shadows, and clink the spoon on the edge of the bowl for each mouthful. I feel fat for being hungry. I move into the darkness of the living room, and each spoonful gathers shame in my cheeks. I sit down near the edge of the glass dining room table and stare ahead of me through the open living room windows. From here in the shadows the backyard landscapes a far-off green and the sun is white. Muesli gets stuck in my teeth.

When I'm done eating, I get up and bring the phone out from the hallway back into the living room with me. I look at it, in my lap, and follow its stretched cord to the hallway in the other room. It's a mucus-beige umbilical cord come to sit with me in my chair. I'm waiting for Nova, my best friend, to call. I'm not sure why I think she's going to, and when she doesn't, my bones sink. My inside head smells like wet concrete and feels parking-lot empty and I turn it to look outside and everything wobbles when I do. I inhale from the hole in my body.

I sit there until dusk finally comes and sets the living

room on quiet. I think I've been waiting here for a while. I get up and put the phone back in its spot. The receiver fits perfectly in my hand, comfortable and hard; it's cool there on my palm. Did everyone go grocery shopping? I wonder what's for dinner. I click the receiver back into place and leave it. I climb the stairs to my bedroom and there, pull the heavy shutters closed and lie down in my bed. Staring up at the ceiling, the early night tries to get in through the cracks.

Spring 1992
172 Rue Alphonse Daudet, France

IT'S THE BEGINNING OF SUMMER. School's almost out, my birthday will go by, a birthday cake, maybe, I'm now fifteen and hard already on the inside, wandering around Aix before swim practice with Tall and Giant Stephane, back from college in the States and dating my sister Polly, and his friend Didier, who knows things I know I don't—I like him because of this. We're in the cool streets, walking in and out of alleyways, under half-closed shutters, dinner smells of ratatouille being made behind them, half listening to the musicians spread along the cobblestones for La Fête de la Musique. The beers in my head make me fuzzy and Didier holds my hand and wanders me over to the hood of a car near La Rotonde and folds me onto my back with his lips and the sky is bright blue from here. I inhale him like sunshine and his long black hair falls into my eyes when I stare up. We drink more 1664s, and walk up to swim practice together that afternoon to dissolve into the liquid clear. All I want is him.

On the pool deck, I bend over the edge of the water and lower my goggles. My eyesight goes dim behind their reflective surface and everyone's chatter behind me disappears. I hang my arms loose down in front of me, my body, swinging them back and forth on a pendulum, thinking of the ice I'll feel on my skin when I jump in. I hear Didier walk on deck and stand straight up and stare forward, the bleachers in front of me go sharp. His warmth walks behind me, his breathing past my back, and he gets in the lane next to mine. I close my eyes in my dark goggles and bow my head and breathe him in. My whole body swells—he is my liquid sex. My toes curl over the edge of the wet concrete. I can't look at his body, like the statue of David, smooth and eighteen, a wet Neanderthal. My eyes avoid him. During practice he kicks past me, in my lane, arms outstretched on his kickboard, his dark goggled eyes staring me down from behind their reflection. And with each butterfly kick he grunts, each hip thrust for me, I'm sure showing me how he would fuck me slow and hard. We pass each other in the lane and my body swells to the edges of its skin. I try to swim without thinking but I can't seem to make him leave my brain—he's spliced into it and, in the water, I try to shake him from out of the folds.

He's out of practice before I am. He's smoking a cigarette from under his eyelids, leaning up against his beat-up black mobilette. He smiles without looking at me, smirking a secret under his side lips, and his eyelashes beat, once, twice, thumping in my young-girl cunt. His jeans hang low and baggy off his hips and he drags his boots when he walks, a strut, toward me. He only wears old black t-shirts and lives at CREPS boarding school for athletes where all the messed-up kids go. Too good at athletics to toss out and too much trouble for their parents to keep home, they live at the sorry excuse for a home and a bed that is the Centre de Ressources, d'Expertise et de Performance Sportive. These are the lost ones, always. He's fucked every single CREPS girl on the synchronized swimming team and is everything bad. My insides drop out from under me and my teenage skin fills up, dumped with kink for him as he comes closer and puts his arm around my lower waist. I lean backward away from it and don't want to. He leans his body and deep-set eyes into mine anyway and looks up at me from underneath his eyelids and his full soft lips are the only thing I can see. I'm so cracked open, I can hardly hear him when I lean into him and my mouth opens.

For the next week I wear the sweater I wore during La Fête de la Musique, and from inside it, his scent full on my nose, I can't focus, the chalkboards in class write silent white lines in front of the smell of his cigarettes, and I can still feel his lips on mine when my eyes are closed.

After seven days, I pull him aside after practice and, near the edge of the parking lot underneath the white blossoms of a cherry tree, I tell him I want him so badly that I can't see him anymore. Tears well in my eyes and my lungs tighten sharp around my throat. He looks at me from behind his deep-set eyes and says, "Okay, Casey, okay," and pets my shoulders with his big palms. I look up at him and want to pull all of my words back into the air tunnel they just came out from. I don't tell him I want to abandon everything I have in me just to have his smell and his lips whispering full next to my ears. I don't tell him how my body swells for him and how I think of him every night. I don't tell him I'm starving and that I love him. I don't know how to word match my feelings. So, instead, from under the cherry blossoms, I white starch away all the red swells I have in my body for him and tell him we can't be together.

Docteur honoré: a history.

I throw my back out the next day at practice and at the end of that week go see Docteur Honoré, who's been working on my scoliosis. He's a nice enough man, small and precise, and he helps me with the pain in my shoulders and my left knee. I like him. He always wears a lab coat. He practices Zen Buddhism and knows how to handle a samurai sword. This makes me like him even more.

Mom drops me off at his office to go run errands. He asks me to take my clothes off again today and so I do. His office is cold and the blinds are drawn. I lie down on the table. He asks me how my back is and it's been hurting so I tell him so. I'm a little distracted by him today—he seems awfully close. He puts his hands on my belly, like he usually does, and on my forehead. I close my eyes. I like these visits. They relax me. He asks me if I'm willing to really let him fix my back. From behind my eyes I say, "Yes, of course." So he asks me, "Are you sure?" And I say, "Sure, *bien sûr, j'en ai marre d'avoir mal.*" So he tells me to turn over on my stomach. I do. He puts a glove on and asks me one more time if I'm sure I want him to fix my back. I'm a little confused why he keeps asking so I ask him why he keeps asking me and he says, "I just want to be sure you're okay with me fixing it." And I'm, like, "Whatever, of course I want my back fixed." I want my legs to move with my torso, and now, every time I walk, I feel like a broken body with the universe holding her waist to her hips. Not connected. So of course I want this. Of course I want him to fix this. I have to swim.

He opens a drawer and squeezes what looks like clear jelly out of a tube and puts it on his hands and fingers. I've never seen this before and I can see it slime clear over his fingers right at my eye level. He walks to the middle of the table where I cannot see him and I close my eyes. I'm tired and cold. He lifts my butt up gingerly, slipping his one arm under me while the other hand enters me and pulls. The air goes quiet. My body goes silver. My eyes go white. His fingers inside me, the office walls swell and bulge, my skin face stretches taut over my eyebrows and my forehead, and I do not move until he is done.

Mom picks me up outside, smiling from inside the car. I get in and hear the door shut. She has green plants in the backseat from her favorite gardening store near Honoré's office and we drive home. From behind the steering wheel she asks me how it was. I say fine. I can feel the ooze coming out from me in my underwear, and when I look out the window, the trees are driving by under the afternoon blue sky.

We have a thirty-minute drive home and I crack the window just a little bit and let the cool air in. We don't talk for the half hour.

When we get home, Mom tells us dinner is almost ready as we walk in the door. I walk upstairs, thud my backpack on the floor in my bedroom. My head flops and dangles off my neck, it's so tired. Fuck.

The architecture of a brain: a history.

When I was little, my head did this all the time—crooked dangling off my body like that. I wondered how none of the adults could see it. So I'd crawl into the large closet with a slanted ceiling and a gold lightbulb that was mine until I could put my head back on. There I'd read all the books I could:

about the wars in Vietnam and Germany, most of the dictionary, portions of our encyclopedias, and I would lick my way through all the adult novels I could find on all the shelves and squirrel them away in here with me and read about doctors making candles out of skin. It was good in there.

My words became odd because the Adults noticed them and looked at me strangely, so I tried to be more quiet and I also drew like magic with wand pens and inks and the Adults thought this was Special, too. I DO NOT TELL THEM that it wasn't my fault that the windows in my eyeballs screamed neon streams of lightning blue and remembered the shapes and lines of everything. The Adults didn't know that my body hurt and hard glass pointed my insides up, so I would scratch my tongue and extend my fingers to my sides and butterfly wing when they would say that I was good! I would put things in straight lines like a window to make the sounds go away and my head come back.

Sometimes, when it's too loud now, I crawl into the bottom of my closet here in France to remember my Louisiana quiet of then. There, I'd close the door and sit in the dark where no one could find me, and I'd write rules and rules and rules: NEVER LET PEOPLE KNOW WHAT YOU ARE THINKING. I'd fold the paper sharp perfects away with my other accumulated little notes and rules about how to go about being in the world and, in Louisiana, I'd tuck them into my favorite white purse: a single zipper the length of it, it would open up like a yawning lip, its minuscule teeth strung to a white thin shoulder strap. It had embossed leather flowers on it that I would rub gently before closing it back up, wrapping the strap around it and carefully putting it away on the shelf in my closet. I'd wash my mouth out with soap when a rule was broken, leaning over the sink upstairs alone and rinsing out, and I'd not look at myself in the mirror anymore. Still, when I brush my teeth, I ONLY STARE AT MY EYES DO NOT LOOK AT MY FACE, and I often feel like washing my mouth out with soap—so I do.

Here in my room after my visit to His office, standing in front of my desk, I put all the books and notebooks and pens in a straight line—there, now I will remember everything—and flap my fingers so they butterfly open twice with my right hand and once with my left hand, like I did when I was a kid. Before the Adults found out how I could see and I was all the time a butterfly, I'd practice lecturing my lessons to my youngest siblings, one day drawing on a dry-erase board the insides of an egg. "This is the inside of the universe," I told them, pointing to the egg. I wish it was still that easy now—just me in a playroom, doing whatever I wanted, learning whatever I wanted, and making the sounds of the shirts on my sleeves go away.

The Adults were so oblivious that the first few months back in France I disappeared the fact that I could hardly read French, despite it being in plain sight for months. That first year, I spent days in the high white ceilings of my new bedroom in our Mont Robert house that smelled clean and white, memorizing the letters that made the words of entire textbooks. On test days, sitting on a new metal chair, I'd look for key words in the question, flip through the Rolodex of images from the textbooks in my brain for the matching words, and write out the answers by rote. I read all of *Le château de ma mère* and passed its comprehension test like this, without actually understanding a thing, and would ace my history exams in the same way through December when my reading comprehension caught up with my brain and the drawings that words make, and I met Nova.

But in that silence of hardly understanding French, I learned the most important thing watching side eyes glaring at Arabs as they walked by, slight side-steps further away from them as they came into class. Invisible and mute, I learned the thing that doesn't have a word but pushes its weight, heavy and mud-like on everything like it did when we lived in Louisiana. In third grade there were two small black girl children who were allowed to come to our private god school with a red cross and blue shield. Their hair was always shiny and the tips of it on their foreheads glistened in the heat and the sun. They smelled sweet like the inside of the raisin boxes in my lunch and I'd watch everyone circle wide around them as they walked through our recess with no one talking to them for a reason we did not have the word for but we all knew. Somewhere in there, the swamp hissed at me and I knew to be nice.

CASEY LEGLER

And so in this silence, this new one in France where kids spoke a tongue I did not understand—this quiet where kids fought on concrete with punches that thudded heads, cracked into the ground with blood and no adults around or who came to help; this place where kids smoked at the backs of the buildings and made out with each other, hard bodies up against walls—here, in this place, I learned this lie of Race, *ta race*, an arbitrary pick of history and skin, and was repulsed, and my body pinched back into itself. The Adults made this. I'd watch the kids walk to the back of the buildings and I'd bounce a basketball alone in the concrete slab that was our recess playground with no one to talk to about this, but when I learned to say it, I did: *Je rejette*. That was the year I began to hardly believe a word the Adults said anymore. If they had managed to lie about this, they were lying about everything. No one around me seemed to care or notice.

So I stopped fitting in behind the polite and friendly manners that I learned in Louisiana and that hid me. I gave up, not knowing how to explain that I didn't understand anything but the way light looked in the sky or that I could see a flower petal breathing. I resigned myself to sitting next to my new girlfriends, wanting to discuss *Du côté de chez Swann* and knowing that they wouldn't—they didn't even know who Proust was yet, all they had were favorite boy bands and boy crushes, favorite clothes they loved to wear and sweaters and ribbons they actually cared about next to my plain ones I didn't care about save for a silk scarf I wore for class pictures that year. They gossiped and got excited and preferred some things over other things. None of this I understood in the light of my newly learned truth: that it all meant nothing but what we made it mean. That said, I was willing to believe that they did think these things important. They cared—I didn't. I couldn't seem to summon any effort for anything but for reading, and this only for books they hadn't read yet. So I smiled when I was around them, listened mostly, and tried to breathe and not show it when the wide, empty feeling that broke open my insides would try and suffocate me again. Sometimes when this happened, my brain would fall backward and jump off a cliff with no ground below, making me dizzy, and Nova was the only one who noticed when I would lose my balance. We never said anything about it.

At the end of that school year and the beginning of summer, I was twelve and learned I could commit a word called suicide. A family friend had told us how our uncle died and I decided then that when I turned fourteen, I'd do it too.

Back in my room as I wait for dinner, I pull out the rest of my books and my notebooks and add them to the stack on my desk. I have two essays to write tonight; I put those papers to one side. Before I go to sleep, I also have math homework to solve and history to read for tomorrow; I make a pile of the math and sit my history book next to it. I rethink this and move the history book to under the pillow in my bed—I've heard somewhere that you can seep information into your brain while you're sleeping. Whatever, this makes it one less thing I have to do.

I'm so tired, my eyeball sockets sting. I don't rub them. I have a German test as well. Back at my desk, looking at all my work, I figure I'll just cheat off of Nova. She and I have been best friends for two years now. She's little, small like a bird, and is the only one who doesn't seem scared or impressed by me. She's the only one I think who knows me and doesn't mind—so I love her. I know she hates it when I copy her tests, but I know she'll get all the answers right, having studied for it, and this means something. Her mom always makes her and her sister sit right down to do homework when getting home after school and always checks their homework when they're done; it's always seemed a little excessive, especially compared to the complete absence of anyone asking me if I've done mine. I thumb through the lesson, distracted, turning each page, making an effort to look like I'm trying, but to no one in particular, since I'm alone in my room. At least with this thumb-through, I think as I turn another page that I'll be able to know enough visual cues to know which answers to lift off of Nova. From behind cartoons of German grocery shopping, I consider that it only vaguely bothers me that Nova doesn't like letting me copy—*das, ein, dem*—I've been doing it for so many years.

I snap the book closed and figure to just ignore the small nagging feeling of guilt at her discomfort over the risk of getting caught. Putting the book away, I figure I'll stop when she gets uncomfortable enough to say something to me. I know she won't and I am fine with that. I look at my watch: it's already 9:00.

Mom's voice calls dinner up the stairwell. I snap my body back on. I look at my work and leave it to go eat—I'll finish it later once everyone has gone to sleep. I walk downstairs to a full house—everyone but Dad is home—and Mom's making something in the kitchen. It smells warm and sweet: caramelized green beans and onions that Dad usually makes. Mom's are soggy and never as good. Leaning against the kitchen cabinets, I ask her back if there's enough time for me to take a shower. Dad walks in the front door and cold air comes in with him. He smells like outside. He kisses her with his soft puffed lips and closes his eyes; she leans up into him, ignoring me. Saying, "Hey, Case, how's it going?" and not waiting for an answer, he sits down at the head of the glass table, his back to us, with a Jack on the rocks, and looks through work papers, his briefcase open at his feet. Without looking up from the stove, Mom says yes, so I walk past Sue and baby Addie reading in the living room and pet Sue's head. One, two.

I click the bathroom door behind me and turn the hot water on. The steam cracks my skin like paper and I can smell the chlorine lifting off my body. I step in and duck my head under the shower. The hot water opens up my face and my insides sigh from the stretch. It makes me feel good. I shut my eyes and let the water warm my bones.

The architecture of a family: a history.

As a little kid in Sainte-Maxime, my first memories are seeing knee-high socks and hearing the sound of sneakers screeching short stops on a mopped basketball court I was told to not walk on during games. The tip-off belonged to my dad, the tallest on the team, and after the first whistle blew I'd be allowed off my mother's lap and would climb down the wooden stadium seats, feeling satisfied because my dad had touched the ball. I'd walk to the edge of the court, staying off the red lines like I'd been shown, and while large, fast-moving men in shorts and sweaty legs ran toward me from the other end, I'd rush to push the heavy door open in the wall under the basketball hoop, like I'd been told to do, and slip through it before the game and the ball and the man players and loud sounds got to me. I got it right every time.

There, in the dark side rooms, I'd play with the boys on giant blue gym mats. We'd have to reach our arms up and climb them, hitching one leg up at a time to pull ourselves up onto them, they were so big. They'd give under our weight and we'd lose our balance easily, rollicking then, our footing funny and unsteady. We'd roll around, not making noise in the cool shadows, the plastic from the mats sticky on our kid legs from the sweat. The dark blue metal beams above us would hush us, black shapes and smiles you couldn't see, soaring at each other through the air, and the muffled referee whistled far away. Dust floated up and caught beams from the sun outside, and we'd fly through clouds of small gold flecks floating around us, glimmering.

At half-time, we'd climb the loud bleachers back into the neon light and fidget, scared by our fathers and uncomfortable. They'd run up and down the court and shout, mad at each other. My father was angry and would go screaming, red-faced, arms muscled and fast, in a language I did not understand. He was down there being shoved by dangerous men and my brain embarrassed would click to the dark side rooms where the fairies were quiet and I'd make the stadium lights shine into my eyes and make it white.

When his team would lose, I'd choke on my throat and get put in the backseat of the car after the game. Dad would punch the car window and slam his door getting in. I'd fall through a hole in my body and disappear into the night sky outside. Skittish, I'd have to dodge thunder now and the empty basket under and around my belly would roll and make my fingers shake. I'd hide them in the seat. His enormous shouts would make my body float away, my lungs deflate to breathe, and I would not move and be the hollow and the heavy. The wheels under the car would hum for me from over the ground below, and I'd feel them under my thighs, rumbling over and over again. My back would sink into the backseat corner and I'd watch Mom in the front next to him, her face staring straight ahead. The streetlights would glow in on her cheeks and nose and forehead, her perfect eyes like a cat, and then go away. She'd blink, and the street would shine on her beautiful lipstick-glossy lips and make them gleam—and go away again.

That night, in the middle of dinner, Dad grabbed my little brother Mert and dragged him to the hallway and, pulling him up off the floor by his six-year-old neck, held him against the wall and shouted thunderstorms up into his face. We all bent our heads down and Mom ate a forkful of food, telling us to keep eating and not to worry and that everything was just fine, as she leaned over the table from her seat reaching for the salad, and asked, "Polly would you pass me the salad, it's so delicious, please." All I could see was my brother's small body hanging out of the corner of my eye. I took a bite and tried to swallow.

War

Summer 1992
A Clockwork Orange en V.O. au Cinéma Mazarin

I CUT MY HAIR AND ONLY WEAR SMALL ROUND SUNGLASSES and striped shirts or large white blouses. I finally convince my mom to buy me blue penny loafers that click when I walk in them. I only wear them with my white socks, white t-shirts, and jeans, fifteen and lip gloss like pale cream even though it's too cold not to be wearing a jacket. I don't tell anyone I'm freezing: a few more weeks and it'll warm up—I can take it. Until then, my skin is smooth like a lollipop, a flower in a fridge, crystallized to hard on the edges—I look good. My girlfriends and I skip class and sit out on the Cours Mirabeau smoking cigarettes. Even Nova is there—small, beautiful, birdlike Nova—she never skips class, so I feel even less guilty for it. I'm glad they still have the heating lamps out.

My back leans into its café chair, satisfied, and after each cigarette inhale I watch the girls chat about the school trip they're taking to Australia. I have to stay behind for a national meet and I don't tell them that I'll miss them. When I think of this, an empty space stretches the familiar ache yawning inside me. I lean into my elbow and my cigarette and look up the street. I inhale and ignore them while their voices fade into the backs of my eye sockets. I watch the sky against the small buds on the *platanes* down the Cours. Come summer, they'll grow and cover the Cours, and when the leaves shake, this place will shimmer under their green lagoon and the sun will flash through it like goldfish. For now, though, they're little tits, nubs perked against the street and the sunshine.

I turn around and speak up, interrupting. I want to know how Chiara feels about sleeping with Mathieu. The conversation shifts to this, away from the trip, and I'm glad for it. I inhale on my cigarette—she's the only one of us who has fucked. This makes her a bit of a whore in my mind, but I also can't help from being mildly fascinated—she seems uninjured. I don't understand this. She genuinely seems fine with it. I only catch glimpses of her cracks when she starts talking about "it" like she's done "it" so many times. We all know it's only been a few weeks. We also all know for a fact that she likes this dude. The girls all shift awkwardly in front of her pretending. She inhales off her cigarette from behind her sunglasses and I take a sip of my beer. I exhale smoke out of my mouth and say that I'm ready to fuck too. This is true: I'm angry at fucking in a general way—the "when" of "it" shouldn't be such a big deal. If I could, I say, waving my cigarette, I'd get it out of the way now, like Chiara. And I down the end of my beer, crush out my *mégot*, and stand up to say good-bye, to leave them, to walk up to practice at 4:00. They don't seem to mind, everyone by now just accepting the fact that I walk the edges of our common timelines, weaving in and out of our space-time together, driven by the clockwork of my practices, leaving early or arriving late to things because of them.

So today my feet walk the cobblestones to the pool again, and the sky is the blue above me like it always is when it's watching. My shoes make sharp black shadows and clicks on the street, and each sound edge reminds me that I am nothing and that my heart does not matter. I actually have no idea why I want to quit swimming and, walking up a side street, I feel guilty that I want to, but I've stopped saying anything about it—it doesn't seem to matter anyway. No one cares.

Perhaps a jesus.

The September we moved back to France, Mom brought me to the pool in Aix-en-Provence. Driving into Aix from the Mont Robert house, on the Avenue des Belges, near La Rotonde, I saw a statue of Jesus crucified on the corner, an afterthought still standing as a monument, and was surprised to see him out. We drove past and I asked Mom if people were more religious in France. She said no and, still driving, started to cry because a fast-moving French driver had cut her off—she didn't see them coming from behind her into the *rond-point*. I leaned in to watch Jesus disappear through the traffic from the side mirror, and then looked away, nervous at the other cars and Mom, so I drove in my brain and told her what to do.

We met the coach, Gérard, on deck and Mom asked him in the French I still didn't speak or understand if I could start swim practice with my older sister, even though I was only twelve. They discussed this from over a metal barrier, between me in my jeans and white t-shirt, and the fifty-meter pool behind him, and his eyeballs went squinty, a smile above his full lips—I see him understand that he's just hit the genetic jackpot with me. I am very skinny, and at twelve I am already just shy of six feet tall—I am currency. I learn this, and that neither of these adults cares about me, that afternoon, when I was scared, and he said: "Yes."

So I've been swimming fast now for the past two years since then and I stroll the city up to practice every afternoon through her shaded streets. My skin goose bumps from the cool concrete on the buildings and I don't care. I turn the last corner and startle, a quick inhale under my breath: They're there. I forget immediately where I've come from. I duck my head slightly and keep walking toward them: The street punks. Their kid shadows crouch and look out from the door stoops and over huge canvas travel backpacks. Their eyes dressed in dirty clothes all the same color brown. Filthy hands, paws with black dirt permanently crusted into their fingernails and into the creases of the sides of their palms, hold beer bottles limp from them. They sip distractedly, eyeing me sideways from the grime on their faces. I walk by and the mutts at their feet open their eyes at the echo of my footsteps. My body thumps in recognition. My heart booms in my fingers like a bomb. They are the lawless and *les vagabonds*—they breathe free and they are runaway trains, stringy hair and dirty shaved heads, I want to be them I am them they are my family, but, head bowed, I make myself keep walking past their feral gaze—*I have to go to practice I have to get to practice I have to get I have to* . . . I feel their eyes on me, like calling weight they see me, and I turn the corner for the *périphérique* and there I make my sternum tuck their stares and fold their wild away like a clockwork orange into my bones so I can forget about them for swim practice. I make my body turn hard—and then keep walking up to the pool.

The parking lot smells like chlorine, even before you see the pool. I walk into the women's locker room and the bleach meets my nostrils, warm and sharp down my insides, and they flare. I walk into the metal cage at the end of the hall where we keep our gear in between practices. It's quiet when I get there, the narrow space already full with the other girls saying nothing. Our swimsuits hang like skins waiting for us until we fetch them and slip them on again for another workout. I take mine off its hook. We work our bodies quietly around each other, putting our bathing suits on in the small space. Mine is still cold from swim practice at noon. When I put it on, it's like barfing cold bile on my skin. I hold my breath and arch my head back on an inhale and pull it up to my cunt. No one says anything. Their bathing suits are wet too.

Since getting drunk at her house when I was twelve and she was fourteen, Celeste and I have become friends. She leans against the metal frame of the cage, waiting for me. I grab my towel and throw it over my shoulder and slip into my flip-flops, and she and I walk through the showers together, without taking one, to reach the pool. I watch her legs, full up to her hips into a curvy ass, and catch my skeleton walking by the mirrors. I wonder when the dip in my butt will go round like hers—I am the ugliest: skeletal—and look away. We roll up the sides of our bathing suits distractedly, hiking the edges up over our hips as we walk. It makes a sharp V pointing to our vaginas—this is how we look good. The floor is slippery and wet on our flip-flops and we say nothing to each other—this silent part of my day: my favorite.

We jump over the foot pool, not even bothering with it—it's gross—and landing on the other side: the pool opens up in front of us. They've cracked the retractable ceiling roof so a streak of sunshine lands in one of the lanes. It's slapping shadows and light on the water's surface. I decide to swim in there today and hope I get tan. Echoes of the full pool, water splatting, people walking past me, running, whistles blow ("*No running!*"), laughter and shouts—all of it flies off the walls, and I look up. Through the open ceiling, spring comes in from outside, and I smell it.

The rest of the team slowly shows up, one by one or in pairs from the locker rooms, gear bags and towels in their hands, water bottles full. They drop it all at their lane when they pick one. We have four lanes set aside for us. The rest are for the public. Coach gathers us in front of the dry-erase board and we can see our practice written up there for the night. It's all endurance work—long, long sets of fucking nothing. My sigh resigns itself to the workout and, shoulders slumped, I turn around to face my lane and the water and the far-off wall at the other end of it. I try to hope that it'll be one of those practices where my brain lifts out of my body and I can't tell I'm swimming. I doubt it—it's gonna hurt and I'm gonna have to try. I snap on my swim cap like a habit and consider the set of two hundreds while everyone talks around me. My toes curl over the edge of the pool. I know I have at least the rest of the warm-up before I have to worry about how I'm going to get through this. I wonder how I'll swim tonight, fast or slow. I don't really ever know anymore, either one being as accidental as the other.

I breathe out and bend over the water, arms hanging loose, a pendulum swaying back and forth. I get ready to feel the cold. I know the first second will burn. It does every time. I dive in.

The Water bristles the length of my body and moves the hairs on my arms, to under my armpits and down my thighs. She licks her cold open mouth down my shins, to my upturned toes. I kick Her silently to the bottom tiles. My arms slowly float from out in front of me, down to my sides, where my hands limp behind me, fluttering up and down like butterfly wings on my hips. Bubbles whirl millions of small and large translucent circle lines out of my nose, and my eyeballs watch each tile pass by, my nose so close, it almost grazes each one of them. I move my black shadow over the bottom with long, slow dolphin kicks. The water looks like the blue ocean down here. I pull my arms up to my shoulders slowly and touch the tiles, passing them underneath the skin at the edges of my fingertips, and I float forward, over them. I slow down to a stop under here and gently curl up my legs to my chest. I am a cocoon. I am an embryo. I am this. I close my eyes and the light shimmers around me. I bow my head, ready to press my whole body to the surface.

I explode out in one long rise above the surface and my arm moves like a whale over its body for her first stroke.

I have breached.

After the drowning: a small history on effort.

As a child, there was my first swimming. The minuscule white tiles in the hallway to the local public pool ricocheted on my eyeballs and walking to the water there, my small padded feet hurt stepping on them—nails pointed upward. I waded through a foot pool, icing my ankles, searing a burn and invisible blue line through them, and I looked down and wondered if they'd click off, so I hobbled to keep them attached. On deck, my body flinched at the sounds screaming down on it from the tiles, echoes of everyone at the pool, and clenched hard against my bathing suit, cold and jagged. Once in the water, my staccato: foggy, burning eyes, water up my nose, choking as I breathed, and the bang of the wall against my head as I swam into it from keeping my eyes shut tight against the chlorine. Head up in low, throbbing pain from the bonk, a gnarly finger pointed at me and a coach's hairy knuckles baritoned that I wouldn't be crying if I just opened my eyes. Until then, puffed up and proud—*I am a peacock!*—I had figured out that my eyes wouldn't burn if I shut them, and found this clever, but the loud Knuckles bouldered "*No!*" and I ducked my head underwater up to my ears for the silence, and there an empty sob. Tears, warm on my eyes, mixed with the cold water and I knew the sky while it was quiet under there.

My five-year-old arm hung its body from the edge of the concrete pool, and I lifted my head, the ground like loud steel and the Furies from the ceiling tiles screeched down on me and whirled and made me dizzy. I pushed off the wall and a skinny arm smacked the water with pinched slaps, and the liquid barbed into my fleshy eyes that I see out from now.

Fall 1992

AT FIFTEEN, I'M ONE OF THE ONLY ONES LEFT. Most everyone on the team when I first started has left for college or stopped altogether. They show up every once in a while and get in the pool with us for what seems like a residual habit, but they usually don't make it through the whole practice, bored or too tired, and leave early. I feel jealous of them when they walk off the pool deck and judge them for having become like everyone else—no longer swimmers, no longer suffering.

It seems like a long time since I was twelve and swimming with the team for only a year. I had gone over to Celeste's house that first spring with the whole team. Celeste's parents left her the house for the summer. We played grown-ups, cooked pasta for dinner, like we'd all done this before, and sat at a long wooden farm table eating it. That night, over the clink of metal forks on white plates and folded white paper napkins, the sun had lingered purple on our hunched backs and a rectangle of it had landed a gold patch on the wall near the doorway and when I looked through it the grass outside—blue.

There, in the loud yellow laughs from the lightbulbs, I suffered the awkwardness of everyone not seeing that I had survived up until now screaming behind hellos and polites, familiar with the incessant digging hollowing deeper into my chest and the vibrato that is my sound and sight. I sat uncomfortable while their fun laughed around me. They couldn't tell I was dying, my skin scratching off the discomfort of breathing in and out loud in my head.

Through the broad boy shoulders hunched at the table, one of the older kids asked me if I wanted a beer. Unsure and unhearing through the noise in my head, I said yes. *I don't belong here,* my ribs inhaled into themselves. The light got more gold and a soft muffled sound started coming through their mouths as I drank. Another drink got made for everyone and I was handed a long, narrow pastis glass and, holding it in both of my hands, staring at its thin proportions and the beautiful iridescent green on the inside of it, my eyes glazed over and the sound in my head hushed. I wondered at that and took a sip.

The TGV: a history in the geography of an esophagus.

The TGV is the fastest train in France and it rips through the countryside at about 350 kilometers per hour, exploding the garigue out from under it. Its alcoholic namesake is this drink I was handed that night from across the table. It ripped my throat open: tequila, gin, and vodka, topped off with crème de menthe. The burn from the alcohol tore shreds down my esophagus and I couldn't breathe, bent over, my hand to my chest, sharp pain stuck all over the tips of my lungs. Tears washed out of my eyelashes—this was god. The burn of it clunked my arid heart into place and I heard it. Each swallow made my body scream at the same decibel of pain as the hardness on my insides, and this filled my empty and a sigh let out from my face. Amen, I bowed my head—the cliffs and crevices folded up inside me, and in that plane of nothing to fall from, I could finally breathe. I looked up from drinking it all and was finally deaf, and I finally understood, and I was finally belonging. They had all been drinking, and this all along since the beginning of god. All my problems were solved that night—I could fly. My eyes rolled to the back of my head, not caring.

I came to later that night curled up against a hard wall in the dark, slumped into a corner between a sofa and a bookshelf, with black around me and no one there but the quiet. A pit of empty settled into my lungs—the absence of the bodies of my friends dancing broke open near the middle of my body. I lifted myself off the ground, familiar with the wind slow-whipping gusts through my upper chest that had come back now, and wandered through the house until I found an empty bed upstairs. I passed out in its cool sheets. I wanted to do this again and again and again. That night I had found the one thing that would keep me alive.

Spring 1993

ONE OF THE YOUNGEST ONES THEN, I'm one of the oldest ones now. Celeste is gone. She quit swimming and is one of the rounder ones who come and swim every once in a while and then leave early—and she was the last one I used to train with. I've been swimming too fast for a year already and have to train with the boys most of the time. And since I'm a girl, I'm the hanging empty of the somewhere in between, ill-placed pretty much everywhere. On training trips, my younger sister Sue, now jumped up to a faster swimming group closer to mine, and some of the younger boys come to my room and ask me to help them roll a joint. I roll it for them but don't smoke, and I don't ask them where they got the hash. I watch them get high from the other side of my room and don't really care. This is between them. With my friends gone, it seems wrong of me to get too close to the younger ones on the team.

Georgine is the only other one besides me still here from before. We both swim four hours a day and lift weights every other day—my own body turning into an object that's not mine, fast and strong and big. Georgine doesn't like me and I can't say I blame her—therein lies the irony that it's the two of us still here from then. I'm talented and don't give a fuck about this thing we're both doing. On good days I take mean pride in this fuck-all attitude, and it stands in stark contrast next to devotion to it: swimming, training, this thing we do on an endless daily loop of sameness. So I just don't talk to her if I can help it, and she does the same thing with me— we have an arrangement. Her hard work and ugliness make me angry because it points out my guilt: fraud. I am not real. I am a fake—a body stuck here in the concrete of other people's hopes for me.

My days are waiting for Godot—I lift weights for an hour or two before noon practice. Having walked there in my flip-flops and socks, I work out alone in the orange metal weight room tucked away in the back of the pool. I spend hours in the weight room pulling myself up and down a plank on wheels, sliding up and down its incline with each stroke until I can't lift myself up anymore. I step off of it and stare at myself in the mirror, bend over as if swimming, and watch each stroke land exactly where it's supposed to over and over and over again—I chisel the precision of movement onto the memory in my arms, the gristle in my biceps and the ridge on my triceps so they learn to know, over and over and over again, exactly where the speed is. I lift weights on metal machines that fall with a clang, loud on empty. The gym mats smell like man sweat. The heat from the pool area doesn't get to the weight room, so I watch the smell in the winter swell up out of my mouth with each sit-up and push-up and squat—the only rhythm the sound of the in and out of my exhales. It's quiet and feels like the dead in here.

Two skylights above me keep me company in gray light and the beige walls with a concrete orange stripe painted on them suffer my blows—the ridges in their concrete the perfect roughness for my knuckles. It's here that I come to know the absurd I read in books but cannot leave, my own Kafka's trial; it's here that I scrape my knuckles, my elbows, for a feeling—here and on the tiles of the pool, punching them when I don't swim fast enough. I have a steady scab over my right hand. Here in the weight room, the growing cavity of despair and apartness that lives in my lungs prefers itself, alone and without distraction, while it digs. It slinks back to its dark place only once I've walked on deck and dived in, the water sliming over me cold and smooth. And then everything gets quiet again.

After midday practice, I head back to school under a steel sky—back to the large concrete building blocks that are Lycée Paul Cézanne. I'm learning Arabic and cheating the best I can on my physics exams. It's harder to do, though, since Nova's gone to the high school closer to our middle school and her house. Because of a deal with the team and Coach Gérard, I ended up at the bigger one, Cézanne: 2,500 students and it's a daily mess of a clusterfuck, the most violent school in Aix. Here race gets divided up in silence across the vast front concrete courtyard. In middle school we used to fight, but now every creed has its own corner spot and from there stares across the divides to the others. From here I'm allowed to go to practice in the middle of the day while the rest of the students have to stay on campus. I miss my girlfriends but I've learned not to care too much about it and it's ultimately sort of convenient—the apartness in my new strange place keeps them from really knowing anything about me anymore and this I somehow like better. I'm usually (always) late for my 2:00 class and I am again today. I walk up the valley of the concrete plaza that joins all the buildings together, and it's wide as fuck—like some large vast concrete desert; I think it's probably what communism looks like. I walk past the theater kids on the stairs; they're skipping class as usual, huddled out of sight from the security guards near the front of the wide school entrance, and smoking. My body has the familiar pang for the freedom I think I see in them but I walk past it. I've shaved the back half of my head and I wear the same clothes every day: t-shirt, flannel, jeans. I know most of the theater kids by sight but none of us are close: either they're too cool or too scared—we never bother to ask which one of us is more terrified and intimidated underneath the tough—and I buy hash for everyone from the one who's always the most nuts. This year it's the shaved head punk with the sharded front tooth, we call him Clébard; he's racist, high all the time and shifty-eyed shaking. He should make me nervous but he doesn't.

I don't fit in with them the same way I don't fit in with the kids on my swim team—the theater kids not understanding how I can be so fast and so good at swimming, and my teammates not understanding why I don't care about it. I'm a border crosser and am lonely most of the time, out here on the edge. At least I don't skip class so much anymore. It's too much work to cover it up and explain back home or to myself and I don't care enough to do it, so I stay in class—blah blah, goes the teacher—and I sit through it unhearing.

Before going into French, I head to the back of the physics building; there's no one there this time of day, and I lean my back against the cold gray wall of it and bend over an aluminum and basil joint to see if it'll get me high, the back of my head, and the natty, chlorine dry hair on top of it, huddles over it and tries to make the aluminum balls catch fire. They don't. I toss it to the *pierres de calcaire* and grab a cigarette from my coat pocket instead. Squatting on the gravel behind the building, *c'est le Mistral* above me and the sky watches me sitting in its shadow from up there. It's quiet back here under the wide. I inhale. We're reading *La danse macabre* and *Les fleurs du mal* in French class. I stop smiling that year and hate myself when I show my teeth.

On my walk back from school after class that night for my second practice, someone walks toward me, alone on the sidewalk too. I wait until they're just up next to me and then scream in their ears. She drops her bags and crouches against the wall, terrified. I stand over her, tall and unscared. I am pleased by this. Tough-skinned, I walk away.

In the locker room for the second time, everyone else is already on deck. I'm late. I put my swimsuit on, unfeeling. I walk through the locker room to the pool, my flip-flops slapping the floor. I jump over the foot pool and half wave to my coach, Gérard, at the other end of the big pool—everyone's already swimming warm-ups and arms come out of the water between us. I step out of my flip-flops and the ground is slimy under them. I put my swim cap on, snap my goggles on, and am cold. The black night of early fall stares at me through the windows.

For Nova's fifteenth birthday that year, I give her hash, folded up in a perfectly small, shiny square piece of aluminum foil. I bought it from Clebard. When she opens it, everyone looks at me like I'm brave and this pleases me—I've given her the perfect dangerous gift that no one else could get away with giving: another metal gate clangs down between them and me, gnawing another layer into the divide I have to reach further and further across to even hear them.

That night at her sleepover party I wear makeup for the

first time and my skin looks smooth like a magazine. Alone on her balcony, with the music blaring from her golden living room, everyone else is inside, drunk for the first time. Here I practice smoking like Stephanie Seymour, elegant and uncaring, with Axl Rose in a bar booth in the GNR music video of "November Rain." I blow smoke out into the night and watch it cloud. No one sees me. I have a swim meet the next day but I'll get drunk anyway so that I can crawl on the couch with the rest of them. And I do. And it feels good. And I am beautiful.

I wake up early before everyone the next morning and Nova's mom brings me to the meet. I might be hungover, I think. I'm squinting my eyes, trying to see through the haze in my brain. It sloshes.

I'm late for warm-ups and can smell the vodka, sweet off my skin—stale and warm from last night. I put my bathing suit on in the locker room and pull my sweatpants up, impressed with myself that I don't care about any of this. I walk on deck and Coach glances at me and looks away. This is what has lately become my cue to warm up by myself, away from the rest of the team. He knows I'm fucked-up. Neither one of us really wants to have to do anything about it, or knows how to, I think. We'll avoid each other through the rest of warm-ups or until the chlorine washes away the smell. The water snaps my skin when I get in.

I go to the diving well and blow ring bubbles out from the deep end, perfect glitter circles floating up—one, two, three. I get out—hardly a warm-up—and drop my bag near the rest of everyone else's stuff. When I sit down to dry off, a few teammates pass by and give me low high-fives for being so fucked-up, daring the coaches to say anything—they won't, and don't. I'm too fast for them to. I like this.

My heat's up. Two hundred freestyle. I walk to my lane. I'm impressed I could even read the heat sheet well enough to sort out which heat I was in. At the starting block, I throw my arms halfheartedly around in a windmill, trying to act like I'm loosening them up. All it's doing is making my eyes wobble out of my face. I can't be bothered to jump up and down to get my heart rate up—I might vomit. I bend over and slowly take off my sweatpants. The air brushes cool on my legs. I just want to be warm in bed. My mouth is dry. I can't swallow. I bend my knees down to the edge of the pool and splash my body with water—communion. I stand up and step onto the starting block. My toes look very far away. "À vos marques . . ."

I dive in and the water feels like lip gloss and swimming in cream sauce. It's so easy. I close my eyes and float big and strong, pulled by my arms through the race. This feels glorious. I am a propeller. I am a tanker. I am a tanker's propeller. I am a large, slow warship. I do a flip turn and everything looks like a fish tank through the glass. I'm not even touching the water anymore.

I finish and lift my head spinning. Looking up at my time on the board: I've swum the fastest time in France. Gripping the wall that's falling between my hands, dangling there, I see the other swimmers coming up from far behind. They touch the walls on either side of me. I lean my head back into the water, on my forehead like a priest, and I watch the ceiling be a clock.

I'm out of breath, I smoked a lot last night, and I can feel the vodka in my arms. I pick my head up and hang my body over the lane line, and it rolls under my armpits. I may or may not drown. I finally get out and feel indifferent to the legs I'm looking down at, walking toward my towel. They go splat on the slimy tile. I can't feel anything. I can't hear anything. It feels good. I walk to a corner of the pool without talking to my coach or swimming down and pass out under my parka. As sleep swallows the weight of my body under here, I hear the echo of the meet around me and want to be out of it like this every time I swim.

The team makes it to the IMPORTANT National 1 Inter-club competition because of my race, and when I'm up on the podium to get my medal, my sweatpants feel warm on my legs and I think about the duvet soft and cozy on my bed at home and I close my eyes while my head spins and loud sounds say hoorah and I try not to fall off the first-place stand when I bend down to get my medal and all I hear is the sound of water in my ears and see wide teeth hanging off heads, smiling at me for having done such a good job. My face is thick, so I peer through it when I walk off deck to finally go home.

Through July, I swim for every chance to get wasted—after every meet, every weekend, every travel trip. This is what I look forward to and what I tell no one: the burn of it down my throat, to my soul curled up in my lungs, the sharpest pain all over it—it seizes and stretches, becoming alive again, and is the only thing that makes sense. When we break from training that August, I drink every day and my head walks off my face until late September. When I can, I fly relief: I get high and wasted, listening to Beck's "Loser" with Polly and our neighbor Lionel, where Cézanne painted at the foot of the Mont Sainte-Victoire, smoking cigarettes while the last cicadas scream at us as they die into fall. I'm a failure and no one knows it: I stare in front of me, at the expanse of time ahead, and feel nothing on the inside.

Fall 1993

IN SEPTEMBER, COACH SITS ME DOWN, ALONE, in front of the dry-erase board before the first practice that year, and shows me the plan for the next six years:

1994 European Championships for finals,

1996 Olympics for finals,

1997 World Cup for medals,

1998 European Championships for gold,

1999 World Cup for gold and world record,

2000 Olympics for gold and world record.

My body goes numb—it knows it can do this and I understand that it will. I'm suddenly sad for it, trapped in this place, a soul propelled forward despite me, and I watch it like a spectator. I don't understand why no one else can see my body floating away. I also don't know how to tell anyone that it is happening.

I dropped out of Cézanne at the end of last year to start taking mail-in classes while boarding at CREPS this year, the same place Didier's used-up synchronized swimmers went when I was younger. The difference between them and me now is that I never slept with Didier and his sexy wild feralness, nor have I ever even seen a dick. Everyone thinks I have but that's because they pass out before I do, and the last they see of me is usually me pushed up against a wall, drunk with some dude. They don't know that whoever that guy is has usually passed out before anything could happen, and that after that I walk around drinking from a bottle for the rest of the night—wandering for nothing that makes sense.

Boarding here means that I swim two to three times a day, depending on if it's Wednesday or Monday—but always at lunch and again in the evenings—and that I get to not go home anymore. I miss Sue and Mert and Addie but the loneliness of boarding here at CREPS with other athletes and feeling left out is more real and makes more sense than the delusion at home where reality gets banged away with smiles and with Mom, wife to my dad.

Over the summer, huge paintings of hers had been delivered to the house, taken out of an old storage shed my parents had rented in Sainte-Maxime when they were younger—before *we* happened. I was horrified when I saw them—where did this woman artist go who painted these wild, fierce, and dark churches and steeples, oceans and storms? Was she curled up in the cadaver of lipstick and smiles that was my mom? Tucked away to better suffer the prison of being a wife? I feel even more disgusted with her for this difference between the passion and richness that surely drove this young painter and the sad disappointed mother she has become. Where did she disappear herself to from those days, and then from Dad? Who was the imposter whose blows I had to suffer questioning my own paintings and drawings—wondering aloud in criticism, "Why can't you just draw lovely things?" after looking down at the news photos of cadavers I had brought back to life by drawing lines and lines and lines over the images of that summer's Herzegovinian and Serbian bodies until they looked alive again? Looking at them hanging down from my walls here at CREPS, I still can't believe she said that to me when she too once painted storms. At least here, in my dorm room, my caved-in insides match up with the depressed concrete walls of the buildings' outsides and no one is trying to pretend they're not bleak, rain-stained, and gray.

I wake up around six now every morning in the single bed in my narrow room and look at the wall, then at a small desk across from it that I can reach for from the bed. I click my alarm clock off. My small porch looks in at me from the still black night outside. I've started painting again and my eyes crawl up my walls, my head unmoving on my pillow, and scan over the shadows of the faces I've drawn—skeletons and dark eyes in here, rotted skin and tracings on top of the dead from newspaper clippings, Scotch-taped together all over the walls, one edge of a drawing up against the next one—like a map of something. I sit up in the dark and—shoulders stooped, my face covered in the early morning blackness in front of it, unseeing—my feet, warm from sleep, hit cold on the floor. I have one green plant in my room with me and she makes me feel like an adult. I flip on the small electric light next to her, and she glows. I pick up a leftover water glass and pour it, listening for the moist gurgle her soil makes when she drinks. I pet her thick, bright neon-green leaves and they are cool and soft.

I have practice in forty-five minutes. I stand up, take the sweatpants from the back of my desk chair, and pull them up over my pajamas—two layers and I can still feel like I'm in bed under my duvet. I put a hoodie on and sit back down on the edge of my bed, my empty feet on the linoleum. My hands look bony next to my thighs. I reach down beside my bed and put on my socks and put on my shoes. I stand up, clicking my dorm room door closed behind me as I walk down the hall to go outside and get to the cafeteria before anyone else is awake.

When I'm allowed to eat in the morning before swim practice, I eat:

1. a small piece of bread

2. two pats of butter

3. a small glass of milk.

I dip the bread into the milk and it tastes sweet. Hunched over the silver tray, I try to think that I like it. Other athletes slowly come in for their breakfast and I swallow my last bite and get up to leave. They'll go to school later at Lycée Emile Zola up the road where Nova and the girls still go. I go to swim practice. I walk past them, waving a sleepy hi to some of them, none of us raising our hands but more than halfway, and when I'm outside I hear the crunch of my shoes on the gravel once outside. I unlock my black mobilette. Sometimes it's cold already and the sun will just be rising in the quiet, and I'll stand there for a second, watching clouds come out of my mouth in the blue dark that's going away. And behind me the cafeteria will fill up and glow gold.

Morning practice is usually just me, Georgine, and Gérard. The pool is closed to everyone else but us. I walk on the empty deck feeling Giacometti in the wide covered dome—my limbs are lonely I think. Georgine is a long-distance swimmer, so she's usually in the pool already, since her practice is longer. I still feel mildly guilty about this. I have no idea how she does it. She's taken to drinking soup out of a thermos during practice. She's so weird. After all these years I can't believe it's she and I who have to spend the most time together. We still can't stand each other, each at opposite ends of wanting to swim (her) and being talented and not giving a fuck (me). Our silent agreement to not talk to each other was made long ago, when everyone started leaving the team to grow up and get boring. It still stands. This is fine, since each of us in her own way has given up—she's drinking soup at practice, thinking this will be the thing that makes her faster, and I'm dead on the inside where nothing grows anymore but long bleached hair and long arms and legs that make me swim faster and become more invisible every day.

Her splashes going up and down the pool, she's the only sound. Gérard and I nod one hello as my toes walk on deck in their flip-flops, still wet from last night's practice. We're used to this quiet by now. Gérard and I don't say much to each other either. We haven't really for a while. I put on my swim cap, tuck my hair underneath it, and Gérard stands next to me. We both look at the workout on the dry-erase board. We know what we're doing. The familiarity of what this is, so regular now, transcends the necessary formalities we used to have. Practice looks numb but I'll do it anyway—I have no questions, so I nod to him, turn my back, and face the pool. My skin goose bumps cold against the warm chlorine air and my swimsuit is still damp on my crotch from practice last night—I'll never get used to it. Gérard walks to stand on the side of the pool, arms crossed, and watches me. I walk to the edge of the water. I look at it, stare down to the end of it, and swing my arms in the silent echo of Georgine's rhythmic strokes splashing in her lane—back and forth. He says, like he does every morning, "*Allez, Casey, on y va.*" I look at him and feel the deck slime under my feet. I curl my toes on the edge of the concrete and dive. For a second, suspended there where it's still dry, I sigh, and the air moves past me, and I'm flying.

The slither of the first water glides in my fingers, my arms, my waist, and over my thighs to my toes. My body weighs down to the bottom, the perfect slow torpedo, a giant and slow-moving whale, and brushes past the tiles with the edge of my fingertips, delicate little sharp points on the bottom of them. I slow down and pull one leg up to burst through the liquid, pushing up hard from the bottom. I Swim.

Gérard and I have been traveling to national swim meets alone for a few years already. We've shared silent breakfasts in weird hotel restaurants at 6:00 a.m. together, so practice like this morning's, long and slow and quiet, is nothing. Sometimes I've felt weird on these trips, just the two of us, and wondered if I was in love with him. His arms are still strong from when he swam, and his chest hair and the strong man smell he always has simultaneously repulse and attract me. He wears a gold chain around his neck that curls around his hair there. He has a gap in his teeth like mine, so we share the same mouth. I swallow around the sadness I sometimes see behind his eyes, nervous that it will fall him away from me.

He's very fond of me—this I know—but I mostly feel weird around him and it's made worse because I know I'm not supposed to. He missed Olympic trials the year he qualified to go, back in '76. He had the fastest time that year but broke his leg and had to watch trials from a hospital bed. He would have made the team. He kept swimming after that but never really recovered. I think the disappointment broke something in him. He eventually married a girl who was a volleyball player at the Font Romeu training camp where they both boarded as young kid athletes—similar to the CREPS place where I live now. Sometimes over dinner he'll tell me about his wife and kids. Nothing in particular, but they always come up. Them and Aston Martins and cigars. He tells me that if he could buy any car, it would be an Aston Martin, and he always leans back with a grin on his face, satisfied each time he tells me this—forgetting maybe that he tells me every time. Maybe he thinks by repeating it enough it will happen. I can't ever tell if he really thinks he'll get one or not. I don't think he will, and this makes me uncomfortable, so I try not to look at him in the eyes when he says it. But talking about it makes him big, I think, so I let him and we sit across from each other in empty hotel restaurants eating dinner over metal forks while we wait for the meet the next day. Me in my sweatpants across from him: prodigy.

He usually gets up at the end of dinner to go have a cigar outside the hotel lobby. From where I sit, I'll watch him sometimes, out in the dark under the streetlight, staring out into space with each inhale, and I'll wonder what he's thinking. He seems lonely and I feel like he knows I am too. I get up and push my chair in under the table, say good night to the server, and sign the bill for Gérard. He gave up everything for swimming and got nothing back except a missed chance he had to watch on television. We wave good night to each other through the glass window. The elevator buttons are always the same in these hotels and I'll press them yellow and watch the floors click by and be sad for him. The doors will slide open and I'll walk down the hall to my room to sleep dead. This is the weight of it. I learn from Gérard what it means to resign to a silent failure and figure that I am this too. Even though no one can see it yet—I am regret.

And after practice, every morning now, I say good-bye to Gérard, ignore Georgine, and walk off the pool deck to the empty shower room. I slip into a stall and pull the curtain closed behind me and turn the shower on. When the hot water widens my dry face, I crumble to the tiled grout of the shower stall and curl up in the corner of it. An invisible howl bricks out from my outstretched neck and my mouth opens with no sound and the rain falls on it. The tiles press up against my cheek and fold it, my eyelashes blink on the cold walls, and my sobs lift up from the inside of my body, my pile of curled thighs and legs in the corner, and tears wipe away everything. I lift my fallen face to the water: Communion. I may die here and I don't know how to leave. I let the water spread on my face and burn until I bow away from it in silence. I have no idea what is happening to me. I haven't spoken to anyone in days. And this happens every day.

When my skin begins to stretch and pulls back dry from the water, I lift myself up, my knees clanking up against the tile; they will bruise. I turn off the shower knob and drips come off my cheeks. My forehead against the wall, I stand there while the shower slows down, drips, and stops.

Alone in the cage, I dry off and layer all my clothes back on, putting on two t-shirts the way Celeste used to, a sweater like the one she used to have, and pull a scarf up to my face like she did, to protect me from the wind on the mobilette. I walk outside. It's 8:00 a.m. The air is crisp and licks my warm lungs. I click my mobilette on with a distracted thumb flick and let it warm up, put my gloves on while sitting with it rumbling in between my thighs, and squint at the morning light that's glass on the streets and looks like ice on my cheeks. I push it off its kickstand and ride back down the slope of the *périphérique*, back to CREPS for the day.

The damage done.

In between practices, I do schoolwork in my bedroom. At the beginning of the year I tried to study in the common room with the few other athletes who were homeschooling like me, but I couldn't stand how serious they were, bent over this laughable excuse of a school, as if it were actually school. This isn't school, this is a joke—I can freely cheat on all my exams now and I do it obviously and systematically, lifting my answers, verbatim, directly from our textbooks and, when I can, directly copying the answers from the answer codes in the back of some of the workbooks. Why they give them to us is beyond me. I'm not sure why I still haven't gotten caught and am quick to hide my embarrassment when I learn that the other athletes aren't cheating too. Why not? I ask. And they answer that they're trying to learn something, to which I say: nothing. In any case, I get my exams back with exclamatory! notes! of praise! written up! and down! the margins and big 20/20's! marked up at the top. I feel mild shame that I'm getting away with this, but mostly I judge the professors on the receiving end of my mail-in exams—I imagine them stupid and lazy for not catching me and think them lame for knowing and not saying anything, the payoff for turning a blind eye presumably bigger than the one for doing their jobs.

So I stay in my room most days between practice and read books I'm not supposed to read. I forget how to talk that year and during Ramadan I stop eating pork like Rahat, the one Muslim swimmer on the French National Team. I don't talk about it with him—I don't want to. The only thing I tell him when he asks me why over a beer on a training trip is: "Shut the fuck up." Over the next few years, when training trips land on it, we'll sit next to each other for Ramadan and not eat and then eat.

On the odd occurrence that another athlete does come by my bedroom at CREPS, they usually walk in, look around the walls at the clippings of war and poetry and skies I've drawn and written, and then look at me sideways from the slit in their eyes, not understanding what I'm doing here—I don't either. By the end of that year, everyone pretty much learns to leave me alone. Not because I'm mean but because I'm the kind of weird that makes people uncomfortable, so I walk like a failure near the walls, to not be too big for them.

The only one person who stops by and stays is the wrestler who listens to heavy metal. He's also being homeschooled and rumor has it that he sometimes cheats on his exams, too, so I trust him. But I also think his coach beats him up all the time, so he and his teammates ride this tight line of rebellion and rules that I don't envy. At least I am the ignored. He and I never learn each other's names. It doesn't matter. The most we ever do is learn a whistle, only he and I know that we whistle call from across the parking lot when we see each other on our way to practices sometimes. He's broken like me; I see the sadness in his eyes. And this is enough. So we never speak much. He knocks on my door and stands in the doorway and leaning against my doorframe on one side, while I do the same on the other—I've stopped touching people sober a long time ago—he hands me a tape he says I should listen to—and I do. It's usually heavy metal. We leave each other alone after these exchanges, but while I'm reading at my desk or drawing, I sometimes see him alone, running laps in plastic bags around the track in the winter time to make weight. This is also why I trust him.

That year, I fall asleep to Metallica's Black Album in

my headphones every night, mostly sad and hungry for Jim Morrison's lips, and Jimi Hendrix setting fire to his guitar and dying on his own vomit, and Janis Joplin's voice meaning something. I watch *Full Metal Jacket* and *Easy Rider* and want to feel the wind in my lungs the way I think they do—I want to feel the good, like them, easy and relaxed, so correct and full of conviction; I want this with all the breaths in my body. The closest I get to this, and it's infrequent this year, is when I get high, but even then I don't want to share my hash and I know that I'm terribly wrong in this.

The only other guy who comes by that year with any frequency at all is Bruno. He comes by to play me songs on his guitar: Simon and Garfunkel and Neil Young and the needle and the damage done. I stare out the window while he plays, wanting to know what a pinprick feels like while he sings. The song breaks open my heart like it did in Plan-de-la-Tour when I was little—I had a pet snail there, he lived under the house's stone bench until one day my friend Orélie came over and killed him with her foot. A trail of snot and brittle shell carnaged where her jealousy had stepped and, unsure whether to cry or not, I went and sat next to the bookshelf in the narrow hallway that led from the playroom to the living room in that first childhood house, and under a white skylight, on a thistle rug that scratched my legs and left small red lines I stared at, I read *Lucky Luke* and Astérix et Obélix comic books. I skipped directly to the pages with the can-can dancers and the big-titted women having their clothes ripped off, pausing for each nipple. My dad would play Simon and Garfunkel over and over again from the living room and it would ghost over me while I read.

When Bruno's done playing the songs, he doesn't stick around. I don't want him to and maybe he knows this. He leaves as he came in with his guitar. I think he thinks I'm sad. I click the door behind him and sit back at my desk and stare from it to the sky outside, waiting for my next practice.

Dr. bastiani: a short history in communism.

I get my blood tested for peak performance every month. My levels always come back the same: an allergy to chlorine, too-high levels of it in my bloodstream from being in the water so often. That, and my liver enzymes are like those of a sixty-year-old man who drinks every day. The CREPS doctor, Dr. Bastiani, is fat and from Bastia, Corsica, which I think means he's in the mob, but in his office his hairy chest and gold chain leans over his desk as he reads these results to us—Mom has come to the appointment. That she has come is no surprise: like the fancy swim meets she only comes to and never to practice, Bastiani is one of the fancy doctors, and so a fancy experience she wants to have. I look out the window while he speaks.

I actually have no idea what liver enzymes are and it seems weird that mine would be like the ones of someone who drinks every day—I wish I did. My mom's waving her hand in the air, telling Dr. Bastiani that the latter results are *surely* those of an anomalous blood test. He stares at her, head cocked when she suggests this to him. I lean back into my soft chair, feel my head lean back into the hard wall, and know that this doctor has no idea what is in front of him in my mother—this human based in another reality that isn't mine or anyone else's, really. So, turning away from them, bored and familiar with this, I watch the light outside change from late afternoon to dusk, and wait to see what this doctor is going to say to this woman who has decided that nothing's wrong with her daughter but, rather, that the medical system which took her tests is flawed. To this, he finally says nothing. He gets up, stone cold, and shakes her hand, letting us leave without saying another word and tucking my test results into his drawer. I hate Mom for what she does and I have no idea why she does it, or what it is exactly that she does, but I do know when she's doing it and I admit that when she does, she's excellent at it. I smile to myself as we leave the office, shaking my head. Bastiani must have been so confused. Outside, walking toward the parking lot, I'm just glad that I wasn't on the receiving end of this one.

It's the weekend and I'm going home for once—it's Mert's birthday—and when we get in the car, I watch her adjust into the rearview mirror and put on a fresh coat of lipstick from behind her sunglasses. I look away before she's done. We don't talk on the way home.

A few weeks later, before I leave afternoon practice,

Dr. Bastiani calls me into his office. It's Friday, so no one is around, and he hands me a plastic bag full of whitish powder from across his desk, telling me he's decided I should take vitamins. Looking down at it, I ask him what kind, and when I look up from the bag, he's already looking back down at his paperwork and doesn't answer me. I look back at it hanging from my hand, limp and full, and look back up at him. He still doesn't say anything, so I leave down the hallway and go back to my room.

The instructions on the piece of paper in the bag tell me to drink one scoop of the powder mixed in a glass of water before practice every afternoon. I walk into my small orange-tiled bathroom from the '70s and flip on the neon light and it buzzes. I take the small cafeteria glass I've been given for this out of my bag and fill it up with water—then one scoop and stir. It tastes gross, I think. But I do it, in front of the mirror, looking at my eyes. Then clink the empty glass down, onto the side of the blue sink. My mouth feels pasty and I stand there. I swim very, very fast that year and I stop wondering what kind of vitamins these are, knowing somewhere that they are the same reason the Bulgarian swimmers don't have minders anymore to keep them from defecting at foreign swim meets, and the USSR is now Russia, and Ukraine has blue jumpsuits, and all the girls' faces are gray and sallow, their muscles huge and winning—East Germany still wins everything even though it's Germany now—and I swim faster and faster and faster—my arms glisten.

I practice, read, practice, bread on butter, nothing. I'm always alone and the emptiness of it hollows itself up inside of me, a warm and perfectly sized me-shaped hole, digging a deeper crevice through my body. I ride my mobilette home from practices every night singing Maria Callas or Queen at the top of my lungs, zooming speed down the *boulevard périphérique* in the dark. It's the only time I'm happy—here in the dark, with my voice echoing like a glorious cape behind me, thinking almost always of Cecille.

Requiem

Until she's not.

Cecille. Cecille is beautiful. I meet her in my theater class—the only class I'm allowed to take outside of CREPS, with regular students. She is as tall as me and has long, wilding red, burgundy hair. She is serious like I understand the world and she knows everything about classical music and opera. She knows more than me and this I like. She casts her eyes down to me when she speaks and I love her. She wants to be an opera singer. And she probably will be. One day sitting next to each other in class, our thighs barely touching, she tells me that if swimming doesn't work out, I could always sing—my body is big and beautiful and tall and the perfect microphone for sound. I look down at it when she says this and tell her I love singing opera—knowing probably somewhere that I never will.

We have class together in an old theater at the top of Aix

and the *périphérique*. It smells like stories and old books. During class we sit around reading texts to each other, we sing and dance in improvised circles in the half-lit space. I get to tell stories without words and only sounds and I love hearing my voice hollow out the back of the theater and make everyone sit quietly and listen. I feel less empty here— in the dark of the theater, when the house lights go off, my skin softens and I am pleased. I am alone in a room full of people and I don't mind that here. I get to travel. I get to be me—full and wide—where normally I sorrow. I get to breathe—and no one knows I usually can't. I've tucked away all the visible behind swimming and school—shadow boxing an "I am fine" for them, the everyones, who ignore the lonely blue circles out from under my eyes. I tell no one the secret satisfaction, the deepest and warmest pleasure I have here onstage. I don't know the words for it but this bliss, long ago made bad with rules folded up inside a purse and sealed with Baudelaire, is temporary, so I say nothing while it lasts.

I don't know how to have friends anymore but out of habit, so Cecille and I don't often see each other outside of class. The last time we do we sit next to each other on a bus to Marseille, having just seen *Waiting for Godot* at the Marseille theater with our theater class, and she puts one earphone on my head and the other on hers and I hear the most beautiful sound I've ever heard, Chet Baker rolling past the window-scape of gray buildings through the seaport and my eyes open wide when she shows me his picture—he is beautiful.

Auditions for the end-of-year play are coming—it's the best story thing I've read since Kafka's *Metamorphosis*, full of hard lines like concrete across my mind. It makes sense. It's the story of Roberto Zucco, a young serial killer who starts his spree by killing his mother. The scene opens up with him climbing along the edge of a rooftop at night as a shadow. He's sixteen. All of us in the class know who this is, we know exactly who he is, we are him, we breathe.

When auditions come I audition for the part of Zucco. He is the wild. He is the fury. He is the danger. I know this and pick as my audition piece the scene right before he breaks down the door to his mother's apartment to kill her. I open the scene with a loud voice, the loudest that carries heavy, and the class goes quiet, the theater goes quiet, the curtains and the beams and the black shadows at the back of the theater go quiet, and I travel, as Zucco, no longer here in Aix, no longer me, no longer swimming, no longer a girl, no longer feeling, I soar—I am free here. I am free.

The scene ends. I've broken the door prop, and my hair is in my face, and I can see the black of the stage floor planks in front of me breathing. The air around me is large and heavy. I breathe. And I stand. Everyone is watching me. I am proud.

After class, my teacher pulls me aside with his wild hair and unkempt white blouse shirt and tells me that he can't cast me as Zucco because I'm a girl. He touches my shoulder and his thick fingers tell me—*You were the best.* He gives Jeremy the part instead, and casts me as the thirty-five-year-old adulteress, dressed in a pink suit who has sex with Zucco in a park while her child plays on the swing set. I don't mind—I know her too. She's the only character in the play that Zucco doesn't kill, and for this—her lipstick.

My girlfriends—Chiara and Cleo and Nova and our new friend Nin, the big-titted singer obsessed with old-timey movies—are the only ones who come see the play when we put it on. They gather around me outside in the lobby when it's over and tell me I was good. This matters. *Really?* I ask them. *Really?* They say *Yes.* Cecille and I don't say anything to each other when we leave the theater: I don't know how to—our friendship is too new, it couldn't bend around the crystallized string taut around me. Our eyes say good-bye and I watch her walk away while my girlfriends keep talking to me, and I don't hear them. I love her. I quit theater after this, like I knew I should, for swimming and for my heart. Done. I quit all of it—the flying, the opera music, and Cecille. I deserve none of it and instead deserve only to feel pain—I should have known better. Another concrete wall crawls over and makes my eyes see gray and foggy. I can't see Cecille anymore and so I won't. The weather is nice outside and the sky, like always, screams blue while the girls keep talking around me and I can't hear.

My eyes snap back. Virginie, another swimmer from the team, is walking up the street from her school around the corner. My girlfriends are leaving from out in front of the theater, for the café and beers. I have swim practice so I wave good-bye and stand there watching them walk away and Virginie coming toward me. Virginie is tight and wears pearls around her neck and sweater vests and moves slow like a behemoth even though she has on high, tight-waisted jeans. She looks like a mom already and her lips curl up on her skin like a Vermeer painting. Her eyes are droopy and her cheeks are a fragile porcelain figurine—her skin that color too. I look at her and she waves—she's on her way up to swim practice. My girlfriend's backs are smaller walking further away down the street, so I ask Virginie without moving, keeping my hands in my pockets, if she wants a ride up to the pool on my mobilette. She stops and looks at me, shifts her nervous brown purse strap from one shoulder to the other, and the purse hits her already fattish thigh when she does this. We don't actually get along. She's perfect. I'm dirty. She says yes. I'm surprised and puffed up so I say okay. She straddles the backseat and holds my waist and I don't see the pothole behind us as I'm backing up. She falls off and in the pothole and looks up at me from the bottom of the ground. Her face has dirt on it now. She smiles and becomes gross so I leave her without saying anything and get to practice late and she gets to practice later.

Practice runs long that night, so I walk into an empty CREPS cafeteria for dinner, missing it with everyone else, just like I do at breakfast. I walk around the steel serving counter to the industrial fridge where the dinner ladies in their plastic hair covers usually leave my plate, wrapped in cellophane like their heads. I bend into the fridge light, take the food plate out, and walk over to my table. They always leave one light on for me and I eat alone under its spotlight, the empty cafeteria all shadows around me. I am so used to it, the empty ache with each silent mouthful doesn't even hurt any more as I swallow. I finish dinner and put the plate on the stainless steel counter.

I walk the quiet halls back to my bedroom. I brush my teeth and pet the leaves of my plant. I look at my drawings and, after pulling the blinds open so I can see the night outside, I lie down in my bed. I've learned how to play the harmonica, and every night I play taps. Something about the long notes makes sense to each sigh. I am so sad and I have no words for it, so I swallow the ache down my throat that doesn't seem to close anymore. I fall asleep until I have to wake up again broken open.

Everybody hurts.

At the end of the year, right before I turn seventeen, I finally get my period. I've only ever heard of tampons, never really having ever seen one, but I know that I need one, so I wander down to the CREPS bathroom outside the common room where everyone still studies and wedge open the metal tampon dispensing machine, reach in, and wedge out a box of them. I have to leave for practice soon, so I kick open a free stall, pull open the instructions while I'm sitting on the toilet, feeling the blood gulp out of me one slug at a time, and don't understand a thing I'm reading. I do my best and shove one up my splayed cunt. It feels awful and hurts dry burns, not going in all the way. On my mobilette ride up to the pool for practice, it thuds up into my insides, pushing the whole street up into me. I change into my suit—I'm late again—and pad my way through the showers onto the pool deck. I'm the last one in. Gérard looks at me from the other end of the pool. I barely wave at him and look at everyone, already arms and splash swimming back and forth, and then at the time. I'll have to start the main sets on cold. I hate that.

I get out of the pool that night and talk to Gérard about the practice halfheartedly before leaving the deck like I do every night. I think he knows I'm crying after every practice but neither one of us knows how to talk about it—we've already been quiet for so long. I stand in front of him and one of my guy teammates who is next to him, their faces wide and unmoving, not smiling and then smiling. I feel more than water slither down the inside of my thigh like a river. I look down and see a thin line of blood coming out of me. I look up at Gérard. He says nothing and neither does the boy teammate. I stand there until I walk away, splashing my feet quickly through the small foot pool and away from the small translucent red puddle I've left behind.

Divertimento

On a highway.

One afternoon in May, Gérard and I finally sit down at his metal desk and decide together, using the foggy and weird landscape of a rationale that doesn't feel or quite look right and smells blind, and that we ignore, and gamble that for my senior year of high school it's best I leave to go back to the States. We decide to follow the myth—the one that's been handed down to me from my dad, who'd been a basketball player at LSU with legendary "Pistol" Pete Maravich and a graduate with a BA in architecture—that, in America, I'll be able to swim. That, in America, I'll be able to study. That, in America, I won't be alone. That, in America, I'll be on a team. That, in America, I'll be happy. This is such a convenient lie for the sallowness of my skin, for the thin paper flesh of my rib cage, that I can't even tell that I'm a runaway. We ignore the fact that, in America, I'll still be there.

I pack my bags that summer. The cicadas are loud and they scream at me while lavender purple blasts my eyes for fields and fields. I smell the thyme and the sea. I smell the sun and watch it leave my head against the circle window of the airplane. Unfolding the picture that Nova gave me of all of us from middle school, I'm crying and the plane takes off. I am leaving and going.

My host family picks me up at Miami International Airport and their chins double up under them when they smile. They are shiny and fat. On the ride home in my first automatic car, the gas pedal gets pushed, then let go, pushed, then let go, and we float imperceptibly saccaded like this down the highway, and it annoys me that they can't drive, so I forget it through palm trees on the highway that look unfamiliar to the sky, and I want to scream, so I don't. Their house sits on the Fort Lauderdale canals, and I listen to you're-under-eighteen-you-won't-be-doing-any-time on my rides with my host sister to school in the white Porsche her doctor dad gave her. He's never home but when he is, he drinks whiskey and slurs words and her mom is tight with perfect lipstick, sitting next to him—this, the only time he loves her. It grosses me out and I think my host sister is spoiled because of it but I let her drive me to school anyway. It's the first high school in the States to try out metal detectors that year, following a shootout on campus the year before.

And here, I speak French with the Haitian refugees—giants come up from the water who are spat on: I am as tall as the black kids and I come from college ball royalty—Pistol Pete Maravich—and can play—and I walk with the cheerleaders because I swim. At first I have lunch alone in the library and eventually outside with my only two friends—the two dykes in school, Macalastair and Kai. I do not fit in but everywhere and no one sees me because of it.

I have a crush on Mick Leago, a South African who lives on a boat, and when I'm home I hold my pee for the first time up inside me and it's weight heavy on my clit; swollen, it feels good and hard and I become sad and empty for him and I rub my crotch in my underwear back and forth in math class still and Macalastair does the same with her beeper set on buzz mode when she's not down in the Keys with her tough black-as-night lover with a shaved pussy she shows me. I don't want to look but I do. In first period, no country I pledge allegiance to is at war in the Gulf or takes forever to move into Sarajevo during a genocide, so I spend that year with my back turned to the flag when they pledge allegiance to the flag of the united states of america and to the republic for which it stands and one white kid runs out of the parking lot after school with all the black kids sprinting after him before the gates get closed down by the security guards, separating him from them, and I watch the skinny white skin hop into his truck with a shotgun rack and a Rebel flag in the back. He doesn't come back to school. I go to church with my host family and their big faces on Sundays and the rush out of the parking lot afterward is more reason for the lameness of it and I find a dried-out toad on the asphalt outside their house and put it by my bed, a flattened talisman on my night table, until the cleaning lady won't go clean my room anymore, so one day, when I come home from school, the toad is gone and my room is clean.

Interlude

I'm the fastest high school sprinter in the United States that year and I get straight As in this joke of a public school, and I am the top recruit for every college in the country.

Seventeen on my Northwestern recruiting trip, I get high in the car with the swimmers who pick me up from the airport. It's dark in Chicago and there's snow thick on the ground. I watch *Dazed and Confused* and don't understand or remember it until maybe later because I am high, I think. We go to a baseball game on Saturday afternoon in the bright sun. I won't go to practice the next day because the snow is two tall walls and the wind is blasting through the early morning black night from Lake Michigan and I say, *Hell no*. This place will kill me. I don't know where that sound comes from.

The next one.

SMU Texas girls with bows in their hair—you are foreign—they smell familiar. White starched collared polos tucked into khakis like Louisiana danger boys but in Texas. I am wearing all black and big deep jewels I bought from the Kashmiri store in the alleyway in Aix-en-Provence after I stopped eating for Ramadan with Rahat. Boy on the starting block because they have a swim meet when I visit and he is rolling his hips to a song about low-riders and cowboys and I am unsure if he is doing it for the boys or for the girls. That night I go to a desperate party and find a skinny boy in the back room with a dirty baseball cap and he doesn't give me enough to drink.

The last one: tucson.

I fly over a komodo dragon and looking out onto its skin from the airplane window the seltzer in my plastic glass makes small silver bubbles that climb the wall one by one and I think of being underwater. I land in the brightest light in a small brown airport with low-hanging ceilings and when I step outside the sun screams at me. The air smells dry. I walk with two other tall boy swimmers who have come to get me and my coach Dick Marley and he has a mustache and is an artist who paints watercolors. He talks in codes

I don't understand but his eyes stop his feet when we step outside and he squints at the light and looks up to the sun. This. This I understand.

Isca Blue. He is as tall as me. Taller. And his lips are smooth like mine. And he has one eye green and one eye brown even though I find out later that one is a contact lens. He tells me his middle name is Oley and I stay at his house the whole time I'm in Tucson there and eat nothing, I am relieved I am skinny this weekend. Isca Oley Blue. I am curled up in his bed and he thinks I'm pretty and last night I rubbed my cunt up on his thigh all night long and he held me and rubbed me and held me and rubbed me and held me under a cool sheet where the light came through like printed flowers in the morning. And we walked into a grocery store and an old man stopped us and, "It's good to see young love," and Isca and I buy bread and mayonnaise for lunch sandwiches maybe for his roommates Shaw and TJ and Tony. The night before I leave to go back to Fort Lauderdale, we break into the pool and climb the ten-meter-high diving tower and fly off of it, throwing our naked bodies into each star in the night sky. We go to practice the next day before my flight and I swim with them, all of them, Tucson, the Wildcats, under the widest blue sky in the middle of nowhere in a water that shimmers, and Isca drives me to the airport and I kiss him and love him forever and I know that here in the desert where the light glimmers I've finally found my home.

My hair hangs wild down my back like white seaweed

now; I've bleached it from the sun and the chlorine. I slit my eyes and they gleam. I get back to Fort Lauderdale, where they still think I am good and I am rotting on the inside. I know they don't care, the coaches, the teachers, that I'm dying. This is from since always. I get high when I can, smoking weed out of punched-out Diet Coke cans behind my host family's house. My hair is ratty and blond, bleached and breaking off at the tips from the chlorine, and my host mom makes me brush it out for my senior pictures. At the end of the year, backstage at the ceremony before picking up my diploma, I recite "The Raven" by Edgar Allan Poe under my breath and then louder, looking at the teacher timing us to step out onto the stage, and she looks at me weird and pats my back like nothing is happening who cares quoth the raven nevermore all in black the fast pretty girl who fits in and is so visible that no one sees her—me—Fuck—This—Shit—and I smile into the stage spotlight.

Olympus

1995

There are no seasons in tucson.

I think that day I got high. Again. And walked on deck
zonked out of my mind and the concrete screamed white
at me and all we did was sit-ups. And the sky wide-open
swirled above me—one two three four oof five six oof seven
eight ugh nine ten ungh eleven ungh twelve . . . sit-ups.

"Coach, hey, Marley, I need some french fries."

"I own you, Case. Get in the water."

And I get up real close to him and I'm taller than him
and I look down at him and my arms are big near him and
I tell him that he doesn't have a job without me. And before
it even starts, I get kicked out of practice again. I am the
only one that semester with straight As and on the dean's

list, American relay record holder. I'm learning to be an architect—like Dad—so that I can be far away. It's the only excuse people seem to stand for so I get to check out even when I'm in public. I am frequently stuck in my studio for "reasons" no one asks me about and I love it. I don't leave except for practice and white bread sandwiches with mayonnaise and cheese. On the other days I eat, I eat only candy bars, because I'm fat and try to throw them up afterward and it burns my throat with bile.

I meet Jake in freshman architecture studio and his tight button-up polyester, wide-collared shirts look like they're *Saturday Night Fever* looking for shoes and his muscles will bust out popping each button down his chest and he's broken and the most talented out of all of us and he loves me and his deep sad eyes and face I don't touch become my best friend who I sometimes make out with late at night in the back of the studio when we're drunk and he holds my neck against the walls like Duval in Stockholm used to when we heard Nirvana for the first time and it makes sense—I forget here. Isca, who I loved on my recruiting trip—his one green and one blue eye—drops out of school and falls in love with a small girl who sucks his dick, he says—I didn't and I pretend I don't care. I don't see him anymore and when I'm alone I cry once over him leaving. I miss my friend.

At practice, everyone else just jumps right into the pool, and I can't shrill the metal water on my skin ripping deep into flesh, so I pace the pool deck back and forth, putting it off as long as I can before Coach Marley says something and I'm the last one in.

Walking back from practice, our lonely feet echo on the same basketball stadium court we cross diagonally in the morning to get to the pool outside. Back and forth every day, twice or three times a day, through this ravine that lies between mountains of empty stadium seats. And it's 5:00 a.m. on most mornings and coming through this dark canyon, up a sloped ramp leading to outside and the morning light, and the ice shines a sliver glass like Christmas on deck and the coaches wrapped up in coats and hats bark at us, and our parkas are warm on our bodies; the only thing under them: a bathing suit.

I show up to practice late again the next day from studio, everyone doing dry land stretching. I sit down and fall in next to Panya, who only reads bridal magazines and looks at me the way weird soup-drinking Georgine used to look at me. Fuck her and I ignore it. That shit. Who cares? I don't understand any of their bullshit and they know it—makeup, fucking bridal magazines: Who reads that shit?—and I look away and I stopped trying to be friendly a few months into the year so we walk around each other mostly silent. I'm used to it. What the fuck am I supposed to do? Between sit-ups and the sky, I think of Panya's fucking roommate, Jessica, who still watches Disney movies and all the boys think she's hot because of some fucked-up virginal innocence and cuteness she still embodies—one, two—it's fabricated and delusional and therefore so disgusting—three, four—I re-main the girl the guys drink with (the girls on the team hate me for it) and I'm not sure if the boys think I'm pretty so I forget about it—I care and I don't even know why so I swallow the swallow and my throat closes up and gets stuck there—oof, five, six—before practice I heard all the girls throwing up their food like an orchestra in the bathrooms, and the coaches look the other way—This place is fucked up—seven, eight—and the sun is the most beautiful gold and I don't understand why it matters that I'm the fastest and Marley won't talk to me about the light anymore—I know he understands it but when I ask him all he tells me is to get in the water. So I stop asking and he doesn't push me in or wrestle with me the way he does the other girls—he stays away and doesn't touch me and I know this means he loves them more and the sky heartbreaks me open and I dive in to get away from it again into the quiet here—nine, ten.

"Virgin Girl" Jessica and Panya and I break the Ameri-can NCAA relay record for the 4 x 100 freestyle relay that season; the fourth swimmer is named after a truck or a car: Toyota. The United States is still in the Gulf after its first in-vasion of Kuwait and Iraq; Djibouti and France are at war; and the civil war in Algeria is still bombing airports in Paris and Algiers for Rahat; and so I stand with my back to the American flag at the beginning of each meet while the na-tional anthem plays, and raise my hand with a peace sign on the podium when we win and a gold medal that means nothing to me is placed around my neck. Marley sees this and through his own mop of hair and beard waves his hand toward me, mouthing, "No, no, you're number one!" and shows me with his index finger pointing upward, waving at me and smiling wide, so I look at it and at mine and close my two fingers and make it one. We're number one.

We're number one.

At practices I keep ducking my head and tucking my mind into the light in the fall and the concrete is warm still and the tarp above us makes shade from the sun. All fifty of us, curved backs around coach, little islands of blue from our t-shirts, and Coach Marley says, "We're drug testing," and everyone flicker glances at me from under their hats and sunglasses, and Brian, who always seems to care about me so in a shrug I think maybe he's a friend, turns around, pretending like he's stretching to see if I'm okay, and when coach reads my name the muscles on everyone's neck shove a little up their spines and I look at the space at my feet in front of me sitting down.

I know I'm testing positive—I smoked last night. My feet are making a hard line shadow on the ground. Do I care? Not really. Just that weekend we'd also had a twenty-four-hour smoke-out. A couple of the guys are having the same problem I'm having at the moment, which is pretty fucking usual . . . What is it that we can drink? Ginseng or elephant juice or some shit like that? Goldenseal and orange juice—isn't that supposed to cleanse your system? We swim sprints that night and Brian and I try to hit 4:20 derivatives: joints are on the line.

After practice, Brian and a couple of the other guys and I go to the drugstore. We buy gallons of orange juice, goldenseal—and ginseng, just to be safe. We don't know what the fuck we're doing but we bring it all back to my and Bella's house, mix it all into empty gallon milk jugs we'd put aside to make bongs (full gallons of pot in the lungs at once—swimmer's lungs—massive highs full push down and get bombed as fuck). The shit we make tastes gross. The guys drink it all. I sip it, spit it the fuck out, and go have a cigarette instead. I'm not drinking that shit.

The next day, I walk in. They won't even let me pee by myself—so I can't just fill my cup up with toilet water. I'm totally testing positive, I think as the pee comes out of me and feels like a rod coming out of me and echoes thick drops into the cup while this dude watches me. Why can't they let a woman watch me fucking pee? I feel weird and annoyed but not really—I am just fucking tired of this shit. Whatever. I stand up, I can't help but try to hide my cunt—but who gives a fuck?—and I wipe, flush the toilet, and hand him the cup, point to it, and say, "That is totally testing positive." I walk away up the black stadium corridors not to Marley but the head coach's office to do damage control.

I make an appointment with his secretary and walk around and around the stadium halls that float above the basketball court we walk through every morning—always dark, it seems, and never lit—and I sit on the benches high above it, outside the gold cave where the coaches' offices' light is yellow and I get called in like an echo across canyons because the entire stadium is empty—holding the residual echoes of its fullness from the basketball game last night—and I walk into the neon light and sit on the couch and begin: tears. Do I even feel anything? I can't tell anymore.

I cry and he puts his hand on my shoulder sitting next to me and I hate it—he has kids and I bet he doesn't want them to turn out like me and he's religious and I just fucked a girl for the first time a few nights ago. She was Shane's girlfriend and she brought me to his house and I didn't even take her panties off because I was so shocked and she could see the nervous but I tried to ignore it—a reclining *Venus de Milo* in black lace I had never seen before and a bra I couldn't take off lying spread on a bed that was not mine, in a wood-paneled room deep in the dark where t-shirts hung dead on doorknobs and a screen porch door I was afraid Shane was going to open and come through. I reached over and leaned in, propped up on one elbow next to her, and spread my arm across and I had never felt anything so soft before in my life and knew I was going to Hell and her lips were the softest and I don't understand why I love them and can't hear anything when I kiss her.

We drove back to the party and, walking in, I heard some dickhead freshman named Scott call one of the track guys a *fucking nigger*. Everyone's, like, *Yo, dude, you can't say that shit* without actually doing anything about it but shuffling around, and all the track dudes are, like, *What the fuck?* and Scott wobbles and falls on the ground on his own because he's so drunk and forgetting about Brandy at the door, all this shit is so wrong, and I'm drunk and walk over to Scott when he falls to the ground, straddle him from above and without thinking, and grab his collar and deck him one two three times in the fucking face and throw his skull back down where it came from. I stand up. I kick him once in the gut with my foot, telling him that he's a fucking idiot, get the fuck out of here asshole, and no one says anything. Everyone is staring. I turn around where I came from and leave the party without saying anything else. Outside in the night I can't feel my face and my jeans are dirty. I won't wash them. I hate this shit. I write a letter I don't send to Mom and Dad asking for their forgiveness for I have sinned and my roommate, Bella, giggles the next day that I made out with a girl and everyone knows. What she and the others do not know is about Hell.

The next day in practice, Scott shows up with a black eye busted face and doesn't say anything and Shaw high-fives me on the side. Fucking idiots. Pushing off the wall, I look into the lane line next to me and Shane, Brandy's boyfriend, underwater, too, pulls down his bathing suit and take out his dick and it flops around like that when I look at it. I shake my head—this shit is so fucking dumb—and I come up for water and my arm feels the air on it as it rises out to the sky for my first stroke.

That evening Bella tells me she can't bring me to the grocery store after promising that she would. I pick up her twin bed and frame and throw it against the wall. It makes a loud noise and goes bang. Neither one of us knows what to do, so I put it back in its place without saying anything.

No one on the team gets their test results that semester. None of us asks why.

1996
Atlanta

I QUALIFY FOR THE OLYMPICS THAT SPRING and on the training trip with the French team that summer, I smoke cigarettes alone outside our dorm windows at night and listen to the mangroves moan, the rest of the national team asleep. I inhale and then slip off the compound where we landed, three weeks before Atlanta, and walk the warm night under the streetlights in Jacksonville to the neon 7-Eleven down the street, into the air-conditioned insides of perfectly organized electric aisles: yellow packs of M&M's, orange Reese's, potato chips—so much fucking junk. I grab a forty, pull out wet and crumpled change from my jeans for it, they don't ask for ID, and then sit on the concrete sidewalk edge just outside with the glow white 7-Eleven as my shadow and drink. The weather is a warm blanket on my face and I look down to the asphalt universe of pebbles and boulders at my feet, microscopic now since every day. I promised my college roommate, Bella, that if I qualified for the Olympics I would shave my head. I can't be bothered to care anymore—I'm ugly already—and (vaguely) wonder why the fuck do the guys get to do it and I don't, so I do—and the next day the only two guys on the team I talk to shave it smooth.

In Atlanta, my bald head walking onto the pool deck for practice, everyone points their cameras at the loud vacuum noise in my head. They don't know that I'm deaf to everything but to the tinsel light that bangs skies into my eyes, and my Olympic parka is warm and heavy like a duvet over my placenta, and when I slide it off my skin the cameras go click and my toes edge the pool deck for practice, I dive in the water mercury lava on my body, smooth and floating.

I break the world record split at warm-ups and everyone on deck stops what they're doing and looks over at Coach; he smiles and is satisfied for bragging. I bow my head underwater, like echo silence folded here in the amniotic fluid, and wait under there, suspended in mid-flight between the surface and the bottom of the pool. I float and look up to the sky through this distance—it tinfoil sparkles like church. I keep falling into the well until my backbone lands, a muffled thud against the cool tiles at the bottom, and from there I blow bubble after perfect bubble, rings floating up to the top while I stay down, and everything is blurry like it should be and quiet there like it should be.

I come up dead-like and my head surfaces through the glass to the rah and chatter: *Good, good, this is excellent, Casey, you have to do this tomorrow.* I know already that I won't. I wish I cared. My body falls out of itself and leaves its skin crumpled up on the deck tiles. I walk back to the locker room without it, leaving it there. My brain swirls and makes a sound.

We hear that if we need to get something, you're the one to ask.

"Hey, Case . . . you coming?"

Do I even know this guy? The next day the bleachers catapult to the pool below us: UK and French parkas, England with Olympic rings and a rose folded on the breast-plates. The light is warm and the concrete aisle-way above the Atlanta sky where we're standing is glowing blue from the Powerade soft-drink machines. I turn around and England rolls up. "There's this party tonight you should come to. We all kind of want you to be there." *Who the fuck is "all"?* "All right, cool, sure," I say without really thinking and look down dazed still to the Coliseum pool below where I failed yesterday, finishing in twenty-third place, and I feel the weight of shame. Say yes. And I do: "Yeah, I'll come."

Through flashbulbs of cameras that night in the club in
Atlanta, heads turn slowly next to me once inside for my
bald head bowed, now listening, England near my ear: "We
hear that if we need to get something, you're the one to ask."
I lift my head to look at him, music loud between us, thinking without eyes, *Who told you I knew how to do this?* And
what I say is: "Yes." I turn around into the flashing yellow
and lights in front of me, go to the bar on automatic. I lean
over the cool, sticky surface to the bartender's ear without
thinking and somewhere near her neck say: "I've got a few
people who need some stuff," like I know what I'm doing.

My face brushes her cheek as I pull away and I raise
my eye to hers and she doesn't move and I don't move and
my elbows feel knobby on the bar and the music swirls
around black with lights I see like flashlights and she doesn't
say anything. She pushes herself back from leaning on the
crud of dry stains into the yellow light like the kind you
find in Casablanca and disappears until the owner, tall and
skinny, from Syria, is in front of me and sits me down at a
table in the corner. My first Arab teacher was Syrian, so we
talk about Ramadan and Rahat and we speak French. And
boom boom the music is loud and everyone is smoking in
the club and a fat man is black shadows standing next to our
table tucked in a corner under one shapeless iridescent light
covered in cigarette brown from the years and I remember
thinking that he might listen to jazz and blues. "It seems you
might have something I want." Turning my eyes away from

jazz to Syria, and the Arab leans in with his perfect suit and says, "Who's asking?" And I say, "Me." Chin shoved out like that, sharp and skinny, leaning back and staring at me. I place the order without caring, and place the others afterward, all night long, and no one talks to me and I sit by the bar in this strange Atlanta, where I was invited only for what I could provide, and one drink after another, everyone just comes back when they're ready for more, all of them gold medalists, and soon as they get their dope they leave and rove back to the color dance floor and I look at my shadow blinking on and off and see my smooth head and look at my fingernails long and ladylike and my halter top and am not sure what to think anymore in the dark boom of the club on this stool, but I know I don't fit in and that I've somehow now become necessary.

Once the walls are quiet and a mop is being pushed across the floor, Australia, England, and I are escorted through the walls behind the speakers. One large, tall black door and we move forward into the dark like a closet, and there's a camera above the door facing us, then another one behind us like little cockroaches on a television screen probably somewhere, and we look up and the door opens and we walk into the gold library—deep red oak velvet and books and books and books lining the shelves: perfectly packaged dope. And we sit on the couches, antiques, and I'm not sure I am awake now but I know we've moved—it's happened. Something has clicked shut here in this velvet back room and the bookshelves arrange themselves and I don't do any cocaine that night but sit hard on the couch and am not scared so I ignore that I should be.

And a wide desk, a thin leather slab covering the length of it—the way they used to have somewhere in America when men were still running businesses and it was still all right—this one has a pile of white snowdrifts on it and a gun to the right of his hand making one small and one large rectangle shape and an empty black circle o, pointing at me. The man behind it says—"Why, hello," and teeth smile bright from skin in a black tight suit and muscles like my friend *Saturday Night Fever* Jake's, opened up at the collar—and they don't hurt me. No one touches me, but when I leave with the boys at dawn back to the Olympic Village I've taken some drugs with me to sell, and I do that morning, and I wonder if they'll stop me at the security checkpoint—it's too early and they don't. I wake up lying on the sidewalk hard gray with Australia's fingers in my cunt and I push him out with my hand. We'd walked back to the Village and tucked ourselves into a doorway crumpled on the concrete still cool from the dark, and there was a green bush in front of me and a ledge behind us and the light was pale blue the way it is in the morning when it's wrong to be up.

I wake like rock and I'm in my own bed, in my suite, in the Olympic Village. The sheets are cold, frozen almost, and it smells like American air conditioner—I'll never get used to how sad it smells. I look up and I stare like dead at the ceiling. This. This is it. The cool white sheet and yellow ember of the dorm room we're staying in. Straight to the ceiling—white. I crawl out of bed and hang my head out the window, the edges wedging into my elbows, and cover my head with a sheet so my roommates won't smell what I'm smoking and below me, every ten feet, a paramilitary officer glances up and sees the white flag surely blowing in the wind, because underneath it every exhale is a cloud like being in one.

I walk outside, hurt and sore, staccato, slowly, I can't even feel it, in uniform for the official French Olympic Team photograph—long linen skirt and red jacket cropped and a white straw sun hat over my shaved head. All the other girls are beautiful like papillons and field poppies because a breeze is blowing and their hair is like Martine à la Montagne and their skirts like the shepherdesses in the hills. We sit on the green grass and pose and I am fat cheeked and all wrong. My head is hurting by the time we get to the dining hall that is outer space, a gargantuan white cockroach landed in Georgia with banners floating upside down from the steel ceiling beams of its cavernous bowels. I have coffee on a long metal table inside while across from me I watch the gymnasts shark the dessert table like some tantric slow dance, every one a nibble here and there, never picking up a thing, and they circle like pods the food they aren't supposed to eat and circle like swan songs on little feet, pitter patter under the white bright neon and colored country flags hanging above us, and I wonder what's going to happen to them because it's the first time the basketball players aren't in the village to fuck them because they're famous and have fans and it's too hard or something—assholes. I sip my coffee, elbows on the table, and then a wrestler comes over under the neon and takes one of the gymnasts away because they all want to be loved and will fuck dick like little babies, little ones, 'cause they're just barely teenagers. And I understand that now some have moved up the food chain and I sip my coffee again and swallow and my head feels better when I do.

Somewhere in 1996.

So when Erik, a new freshman from South Africa (where world records and swimmers didn't count until apartheid's end two years ago) shows up to school in Tucson that following September, he looks at me when the guys bring him over to my house and says in recognition, "Oh, you're Casey." I nod without answering. Did I sell him drugs in Atlanta? He, too, is an Olympian, and I wonder if he, too, is a failure. I don't ask and know that because of it I am suddenly important. From where I was sitting he'd come in and seen the shadow that was in the chair wearing a Marilyn Monroe wig to cover my bald head and I have sunglasses on and he shakes my hand and I don't get up because part of the deal for another twenty-four-hour smoke-out is that

I not get up from my chair. I make the rules—I do it for all of them. Drink.

We make all the freshmen drink one hundred shots of vodka that night for hazing and all the girls shave their vaginas and with their mouths pick cherries hanging off the dicks of the freshman guys. The vodka winner has a bucket next to her to throw up in as she keeps drinking shot after shot after shot: she wins and doesn't die. The cops come, blue lights whirling, and I'm trying to drown myself in the bathtub at the end of the hall when they do, the water overflowing, I've locked the door and Bella tells them everyone is of age but we still get a red sticker on our door the next morning saying we're on probation. We live on the couch when we're not at practice, music a loud and twirling kaleidoscope, and in the kitchen Bella is on her knees doing a Zima beer bong because it won't make her fat and only the boys around her, fists raised, whooping. It all feels like metal. And she'll have sex with Jessie, who moves in with us that month, and I can hear her through the wall and I sit next to it on the floor in my room and the swamp cooler goes on and off click and I paint blue, green, and light-blue translucent little bodies on paper waiting to float away.

I have practice that afternoon and Marley pulls me aside while everyone else leaves the pool ledge for the next swim set, and looking down at me from his deck chair at the edge of the lanes, my one arm hanging out of the edge of the pool, says that I need to shape up or something. I can't hear him—

the light is too bright—so I squint and push off on my back underwater, and when I come up for air I slowly raise my middle finger at him with my first stroke and flick him off as I swim away. I do a flip turn and a plastic chair barely misses me flying from his hands. I get kicked out. I don't blame him, I guess. I don't care. As I'm leaving I tell them they should be happy I even showed up at all, fuckers, and Marley yells something, but the other coaches are already holding him back and telling me from over their shoulders to get off the pool deck.

Still.

That December when Tony, one of Isca's friends, comes to visit from dropping out, Isca comes out with us, because he's visiting, too, from Seattle and the brown-haired girl who sucked his dick when I didn't, and my insides are cool enough to be friends with him now—I don't care since he broke up with me freshman year—and the white powder up my nose makes it better when we all go out to dinner and I get up over and over and over again to go to the bathroom while they all stay seated on the outdoor picnic tables at the Mexican restaurant, and when I come back and sit down we all pretend that I never left and we drive that night through the black together to Shaw's house and the tar in the fridge at Tony's is wrapped up in aluminum foil in the freezer perfect like that delicious and Isca stays somewhere else and I miss him and Shaw comes a drip-thin puddle of cum on top of me even though I'm supposed to be there with Tony maybe so we don't tell him even though the next morning he knows and the air at practice that morning smells sharp like a new Christmas. I drive home afterward in the night feeling nothing on the inside but Shaw's weight on my chest so proud that he didn't stick his dick inside me. I'm dirty, maybe, and write a note saying I'm done and there's a kitchen knife in the silver glow from the moon and I take it by the handle and sit at the dining room table and it slides across from me to the seat where we had the twenty-four-hour smoke-out as Marilyn on a couch and the plant that was growing mushrooms in it because the house was so dirty and the bongs on the floor and the time I had woven something there in that corner for my fibers class at school when I was still going because I'm not that often in class anymore, and we had watched football and I had smoked black night like this little blade against my wrist and dig.

And then my older sister, Polly, comes out of my bedroom that midnight because she's here from France to come get me because I told my parents that I was hearing shadows and she takes away my silver glint and brings me to my bed and wraps my bloody gnarled wrists and we leave Tucson the next day after hiding all the sharp objects in the expensive hotel we stay in before the flight we take to go back to France the next day, and this for the first time of two, for France, still swimming, with scars and everyone only barely looking at them and then not.

1997.

In Paris with my French team for the semester, I've swapped the desert for gray scale buildings and rain, time off to make the noise go away from my head. I stay in the City of Light, not going back down to the South of France except for the holidays, where the scars on my wrists are ignored and my hair combs back lovely, growing out from being shaved, and everyone pretends I'm all right and not back because I tried to kill myself—so I forget I did too. In Paris I walk around in the overcast: keeping my head down at the Trocadéro, looking up only in February when it's raining out and the plaza is vast like the concrete desert in high school, eyelids blinking at each drop that seems to make sense, head tilted to the side with mirrors on my eyelashes. I stand there for comfort. The tourists never come here this time of year so I like it—a vista and lonely. There is space here. I swim and win medals and throw them in the bottom of my closet where they go clank and think of the ladies of the night of the Bois de Boulogne and go home to my Paris host family every evening for dinner and lie in my bed at night and watch the day fall behind the window glass.

That spring, training in Vittel with the French team, after dinner and drinking rounds with the guy swimmers at the bar, I walk back to our hotel drunk with Gregory. I go to his room because he looks like Elvis with a pompadour and soft skin, soft and tight like *Saturday Night Fever* Jake—

his muscles stretched across his skin, he drinks like me and smiles warm full lips, looking down to the ground, so I like him. The walls of the hotel hallway hear our hands on them and they float on the paint to his room. While kissing my face back onto his pillow, after I hear a knock on the door, he asks me if David can come in too, and I say sure and they are both in bed with me and it's black and dark and brown and flying in and out and they laugh somewhere in there when I put my hand to my cunt when David tries to put his flesh-hard penis in me and I haven't had sex yet so the last thing I remember I tell them and it browns out "No" to them laughing above me and my hand can't find in between my legs anymore. My back feels the sheets rough against it.

White morning. Hello. I wish I cared. In Gregory's bed. He's up, getting ready for swim practice. I wonder what happened. The blinds are open and the sky is hello. He looks at me and I lift myself up and I am sore and hurt and when I move it's wet in between my legs and I look down and there is a stain of blood on the sheets and without raising my head I ask him what it is. Why would I bleed? Why would I bleed just that stain? And he looks down at me, our eyes are broken, and a loud clap bursts and I can't take my eyes off the circle that is my life in between my legs and he goes to practice that morning and I walk back to my room, skipping practice; what are they going to do about it, anyway?

I shut the door behind me and with a click the air vacuums out of this hotel room. The chair is worn brown and the fuzzies on its seat are Technicolor, blinds drawn, a wedge of white triangle from the slit in the window lands on the blue hotel sheets and the edge of the white pillowcase.

I sit in the shadow, and with the plastic knife near my bed from breakfast a couple of days ago, rip into my wrist where it might hurt enough, if I can get it to be hard enough until it gives me the sigh. The bathroom light is on and echoes ochre into the room and the white plastic knife ribs back and forth, specks of burgundy blood and grated flesh stuck to it, over and over, until my younger sister Sue comes into my hotel room, sent on the training trip to watch over me, and puts the knife aside and puts me in bed and opens the blinds and curtains and lets the sky fall in and I go to sleep until practice that afternoon.

I still smell like alcohol. I stretch and hardly move. I am not sure where my head is and everything is muffled the way I need it to be. On deck, at practice that afternoon, a ghost. *Stand on the pool deck, Casey,* I tell myself—stand there and look down in between the flesh of softness on my inner thigh, black-and-blue bruises crawling up a dark ocean storm to disappear behind my bathing suit, scabby crevices on my left wrist and my coaches behind me. I hardly turn my swim-capped and black-goggled head to look at them when no one asks me if I'm all right. And I dive—

Into the cold under there like hell burning ice on my flesh, passing hot silk wet over my body and making me clean, searing pain from the top of my head to the freeze that are my feet every time they move a wave out from under me, driving me forward.

I have sex for the first time that next week with one of Sue's friends who's on the same training trip, and his dick in my mouth soft, hard, smooth, and I love it. I tell him I've never done this before and he feels hard and good inside me and he laughs at me from on top of me inside my vagina when I say this and something clicks like a metal clanking in the back of my head and I realize he doesn't believe me and I ignore that he doesn't because he is nice. Neither Gregory nor David will look at me in the eyes, and when Rahat sees me that night over a beer—"Aw, Casey it's not that bad, not worth that," pointing to my wrists, and I guess it's not—he buys me a beer. When I come through Paris on my way to Brittany that summer, Gregory lets me stay in his dorm and he doesn't touch me so we sleep side by side that night in a coffin single bed and he tells me when he wakes up that he doesn't know why I'm there with him.

Wherein.

I find the kids from Brittany that summer in the port of Brest: Duval, Laurent, the Stockholm gang—their home turf and the frenzy with which we fight the night here; the lights at Le Bleizi Mor, their favorite bar, a warm fire against the dark winding streets. I can breathe the salt air here and I sleep soundly with the ocean going back and forth and back and forth so close to the cliff edges of the city.

I'm here with Duval again, still strong and birdcaged sternum sticking out like a proud rooster, his hands and fingers stronger than the ones that had held me up against a hotel wall when we were kids; his best friend, Laurent; and Laurent's sister, Mirabelle—all swimmers, all from the get-down years ago in Stockholm. We've seen each other since then but that was always the first one—and now this one the yellow light of the bar harsh, every window looking out to the sea: a black square. The lines of wooden bar tables and chairs soften with every beer and the walls glow yellow—the fishermen gone now after coming back from the sea, only the young ones left here in the music late at night. I sit close to Mirabelle and gaze into her neck covered in her long red hair. and put one fingertip there to touch her skin gently, a few strands of my stringy brown hair falling into my face from the whiskey. I follow her into the bathroom bar when she gets up to go pee and when she turns around to close the door behind her I put my foot there to block it and corner her on the stall wall near the toilet, pushing her up against it hard and kiss her there for the first time and it's just us and she feels soft and she feels good and she gives out from under me.

When we get back to her house, I wander from her bedroom up to her brother Laurent's bedroom and I let him put me up against his bedroom wall, vaguely not sure how to have sex with him, because Duval is with us, too, so Laurent just holds me up against the tile in his bathroom and I wrap my legs around him, and we are both too drunk for more and I know they won't hurt me and Duval watches and this means that they like me so I love them for always. We are all on break from swimming for a month and I feel sad to leave them the next day before the port festival at the end of the week for a trip around Europe with my old friend Nin from being kids at Lycée Paul Cézanne and her trip to Australia from over a café where she learned she could show her big fleshy tits for cash money so she can sing and I can sit down next to how desperate she is.

Getting closer to here we are now.

And the flowers shoot up for me this summer on trains and I travel around on steel tracks, hum to London with a Europass and land off King's Road and I pee in Hyde Park where I meet Nin and she watches and smokes a cigarette with her hands lazy on her wide hips and then looks away. I walk up the hostel stairs when we get there, dust on the windowsill, the landings like periods to sentences in the climb, and on the fourth floor, "Hello, brother and sister, where are you from?" "Wisconsin," say our two roommates. "Why are you here?" and I don't hear them. I am already high.

The sun lights bright into this place that is the middle of a hope and out on the stoop I see a Her walk by every day with long hair down her back—a Her because she knows something I want. I hustle for change in the hot streets pretending to be pregnant for drink money. Like a specter She rises up between Nin and me while we sit out on the stoop stairs coming in from wherever she's been all night. We're told She's been staying here, in the hostel for over a year now and the black man rolls up in his BMW every day when the sun is in the middle of the sky and from the stoop we watch him go into Her room with a briefcase and brown sugar. All shallow water on my insides and gold white bright smile he gives as he floats by. We watch Her open the door hello, hardly saying anything, seeing only a shadow and not Her teeth—and She lets him in every single time. Her long hair coolly closing the door behind them.

That night I have my sandals in my hands and Nin and I are where it's loud and white and blue and spiked and I drink some heaven in white pills and float away to the boat and a smooth girl-skin on mine walks on me and I kiss her until she leaves and everyone's gone, and I'm barefoot in my skirt and I've lost my shoes and I'm in a car with the bartender heading to South London. At his place, I spread my legs and two pumps and he's done, penis shriveled up in a condom on top of him like a tortoise exposed belly up. I look through his stuff, half-asleep, half-awake. I find his dope, take half, and wrap the rest back up for him. I put my panties on after finding them from among the clothes on his bedroom floor and get my skirt and shirt on:

1. remember that I'm barefoot

2. take note that I'm in South London, and

3. have a vague memory that this part of London isn't safe.

Walk downstairs and stand in front of the kitchen from behind a grate they've put up to keep in their pit bull. I need to get some food. I stand there for a second.

It's cold. I need some food. Nin, back at the hostel, probably does, too, and then I forget her and slip my hand over the fence guard anyway and open the fridge right by the door, grab the white loaf of bread that is nearest, and pull it toward me, closing everything behind me, and slide my bare feet across the carpet to the front door and out.

Dark moon out still and I sit crouched in a doorway in the shadows until dawn happens, hard bricks against my face and wide-open eyes there, small because I don't want anyone to see me, and the night buildings in front of me are indigo. The bread in my mouth goes mush. I eat small crumbs of it until they paste soft in my mouth and I swallow. The sky lightens and stretches with a few strange chirps from a tree on a bird, and I look up and it's blue morning. I stand, straighten the dress, and take a left quietly down a blue alley to what looks like a main road ahead because I just heard a car drive by: door opens—out comes all black, all suited in yellow, followed by all suited in red, followed by all suited in purple, and they've seen me now already so I freeze. They stop talking and stare at me: Jamaica. "What are you doing here?" and I pretend I don't care: "Looking for King's Cross," I say. They glance at each other, shift weight, and lean back and stare at me from above their eyes. I can't not look at them, head to the side, eyes slit to glance. I have no shoes on. I can't outrun them. I don't have enough dope on me to knock out before anything happens. The last hit I took is too long ago for me to be feeling anything but faint rumbles of skin beginning to thaw and have human in it. So I stand there until one of them walks one step closer to me and squashes my cheeks together with one hand, pulling my neck and my dangled body up to his face and I'm used to it, and he says, "You're going to walk down this alley to that street over there and there'll be a cab coming soon and you're going to get in it and never come back to this neighborhood, you understand?" I nod, thinking, *Whatever, assholes,* and still make scared in my eyes so they can't tell—I can hardly feel anything anyway when he lets my face go.

Out from the alley into the street by the dead store windows, I sit on the concrete curb and wait. A kid, strung out and scabby, asks why I'm out here and I head nod to the alleyway and tell him, "Those guys told me to wait here." And he looks down the alley and shifties, gets up quickly from sitting down and asks if I have any dope on me and the gas station across the streetlights up neon white because it's open now and I say yes and hand him some and eat a slice of bread and the car pulls up and I get in. I've been nice today.

The leather warm already from the summer morning and the sky is waking up, I fall in and out of sleep in the cab on my way to King's Cross and the cabdriver and I float over the river and past Hyde Park, and we are there and I am back at the youth hostel in front of Nin and her warm fat tits and she says she was worried. I say nothing and give her the bread. That afternoon I let the briefcase like a magic man into our room and when he opens it, I see every size of little sparkle spoons of little pills, a briefcase full of magic. One greedy hand dives in, the other looking for money—and they take me to Saturn's rings until I wake up in Amsterdam. We are there. Amsterdam. Not remembering if Nin and I got on a train to here from London. Did we? I eat three hash pound cakes and watch the sun set from a window out of which I take one picture and I still think I'm in London—*How did we get here?*—until I realize that I'm not near Hyde Park anymore and look at the steeple outside this window, walk down for french fries in a paper cone drizzled with mayonnaise and holding it like ice cream, an angel on a bicycle with white dreads and a dress says she's seen me around and looking down at the small child she's holding asks me if I want to live with her and the flowers in her basket are beautiful: How do they stay put like that in the basket? And I know I'll disappear here if I stay and I say no and I'm not sure why and eat another french fry, the mayo creamy in my mouth while I stare at her, and I am on the train away from the girl and her bicycle after only a week maybe, who knows, back to Paris, and Nin is there with me somewhere in the next seat with her small waist. I break open after eating my last hash cakes in between Amsterdam and Paris and hers, too, because she couldn't, it was too much and the train car walls become strawberry rhubarb jam and the train ceiling like the sun, the windows frames showing us fields outside, and we call my dad from the Gare de Lyon in Paris when we arrive there that afternoon and ask him for money to fly us home to Provence and horseflies and heavy smells of summer because we may not come back otherwise, we don't think. He sends it, so we buy our tickets and when I get home no one talks about where I've been or why I suddenly came home even after the cicadas stop singing weeks afterward and the weather isn't as warm, and I'm packing my bags again for Tucson to swim under the blue sky there again, to swim again with gashes in my wrists now deeper, wrapped behind white bandages like handsome bracelets. And when I arrive, Tucson is Dry and Desert and Scars and I land there and I am better now and no one asks me about it.

Jesus the lord and savior.

Two weeks back in Tucson and I am sitting across from a new him, *Saturday Night Fever* Jake's roommate, and he asks: "Have you ever done cocaiiinah?" Slow saliva lip-licker close-up his teeth gnarl. Never, but I say yes, and it happened just like that: one line laid out, cut at the edges like a cliff, and I prayer my head down to the table and when I come up for air I am free and this is god again. Where have you been? Across a card table knees up hairy legs spread wide under white long basketball shorts and a white t-shirt bulge where that stomach is—I want more—white socks up to his calves and Adidas flip-flops—I am home again.

Somewhere near the end: 1997.

That September, before practice, I leave a bag of dope in the bushes outside a Tucson 7-Eleven because a cop is rolling up on us. I do the "thing": look the other way, slip your hand behind your back, dig a hole, and tuck the bag in the dirt, fucking hope he doesn't find it, slowly get up, walk away, and fucking hope it's still there when you come back for it. I sniff that magic up my nose and don't go down for days and instead feel the weight of the empty ghost truck on idle settle in the middle of my chest. In South Tucson, a cholo looks at me and says, "You in tha wrong hood," and the light is white like it gets when I need to get out of somewhere. I get in my car and sit there for a second facing a gas station and the seat is burning my thighs because it's 100 degrees outside and that island of neon drips away as I pull out and drive back to the side of town where the houses have glass in the windows and I know the streets and I'm not sure how I got to where I'm coming from. The road streams white line strips and asphalt rectangles and the sky whispers a blue-gray stare at me from inside the car, and the windshield is my picture frame. I pee in the car driving home that day. I'll stare at the stain later on the car seat and wonder at the pile of ashes at the stick shift, and grab a t-shirt from the back-seat and bend over, dab the wet spot, thinking I should start using the ashtray when I smoke. I hear kids playing up the street and when I look up they're slow-motion silhouettes on the gold dust horizon of 6:00 p.m. I take a picture of their zoetrope shadows and slowly turn and stare at the seat.

I leave my car and cross invisible to the side of my house that's shaded and look across the street at the sun burning shadows into everything. The light. The light's too fucking much and the sky too fucking wide.

Jake walks out of the house with his blue bathrobe—I look up at him from my legs huddled on the ground, glad to be back with him, and it's hot outside and we're slow moving from the light, it might kill us so we scurry slow and shuffle from our spot on the ground to stay in the shade. Neither one of us is in school anymore. I dropped out in December,

I think, I can't remember. I just left, not going one day. He says he still goes every once in a while, but who cares. I forget that life before this one. So I look up at him from the ground as he walks out in his blue bathrobe and standing in the shade says, "Smoking Parliaments is like smoking silk." He likes to strangle me when I'm sucking his dick and I feel bad that I don't mind. It's just a necessary. He tells me I don't have to let him fuck me up the ass and I don't tell him I'd rather do it over the couch or somehow from where I feel like I can see him. I squint at him when he walks outside and an airplane flies through the high blue sky behind him.

When I met him in our architecture studio my freshman year he was broken and far away so I loved him because I knew how. Now I clean up his shit at night when he passes out and he won't let me cum because diarrhea is on the bed from being drunk and it smells and I ignore that it does because he is Jake-the-Right, and he throws me a quarter the next day for sucking his cock on my knees while he strangles me. This is the first time he pays me what I'm worth. And I wonder leaving his house if he's actually still in class because he still has vellum drawings of house plans up on his walls from architecture studio. I'm pretending that I'm in art history class, on my way to a conference in LA, I think this is what I told Mom and Dad, and my insides ache again so I get up, finally out of the white sun where I've been sitting. I go inside Jake's house and harvest snow from the shadows, not wanting to make the ghost call, but I do and they come over later at the 5 o'clock sad glow light time in the fall when all the sky wants to do is break my heart. I swim one more time that afternoon. I tell Marley I wish it was different and I feel him watching me as I walk off the pool deck. He doesn't come after me.

I find Brie, a new girl, somewhere, I can't remember where, and she's in my living room sometimes stringy and greasy with dreads, and after getting high and staring at her metal spoon in the shower where she shot up, I'll pull out my photos from the Olympics and tell her about it and do more cocaine until I don't care anymore that it hurts to look through them. I go over to her parents' house once and I learn about pawnshops and what suspicious adults look like looking at me and we listen to Sublime in her bedroom even though he's dead already and never lived to hear his songs. I wish I could die, too, but I put away the photos in the box I keep them in, do one more line, and lean back against the bed frame.

Deliverance.

"I need your drinks." "I'm sorry?" "*I need your drinks.*" 6:00 a.m. She has blue hair and a vest with patches of the fifty states and I stare at her and she is in Technicolor warbles and then clunks back to life—crisp like glasses on—and she says: "I need your drink." So I hand it to her and she puts it under her side of the bar and looks at me without moving, the way people look at me now, through squints, and says that I can have it back in an hour. Tucson law: dry city, 6:00 a.m. to 7:00 a.m. Elbows on the bar head holding up, I say okay and slowly turn my head to my right and there is Jake and everything is the echo and everything is glowing like stoplights and flesh sweat because it's hot. I feel I'm moving slowly, how many days have I been up? There were sparkles in the ceiling from twinkle lights and everyone rolled underwater muffled between the noise in my ears like a vacuum. And she took my drink and I stared at where I couldn't see it and she had put it. I get up slowly like a stork in a miniskirt and heels, some sort of bracelet, short hair still crop top from being shaved, and right hand holding the stool I've left to steady myself like a gold dancer in a no-one-sees-me. Belt waisted and one leg on the stool, the other grounded, and my butt trying to gather itself from the edge where I've moved it so that I can stand up. *Steady.* Everyone is trying to live here tonight and no one is watching and I know that in the thick silence in the loud music and tinsel, a muffled blanket walls me from everyone. *Steady.* Slowly get to both of my feet. And the bar lady—she is sixty and still has my drink.

Getting in here, Jake fought with the cholos outside and had thrown one *blam!* to the ground and punch, punch, the crack echoed loud like it isn't supposed to when concrete hits a head and the cars were all pulled up and a few people were outside and the white beam from the streetlight made them sharp shadows against the cool blue night, early morning air clouds coming out of their mouths from the cold and everyone's shadow wide and big like their coats, oversized to hide the stuff. And where were we, this place that opened only with a metal door and had no sign outside?

That morning in the backseat of the car driving away and going home, my head leans back to stare at the blue sky driving backward through the rearview window. I'm staring into the Universe from here. The time between the bathroom and now, disappeared from then, passing time an art form and swirling still, the growing empty will claw its way back into my chest cavity sometime starting this afternoon. I have the rest of the morning at least until this and my head sways side to side watching the telephone lines above me—a free day absented from time because that is the point—until I back crawl into the crevice inside me and hope that eventually it will be the last time I feel nothing.

Who was driving that morning? The crunch of the golden morning gravel under my feet and the shadows of the cactus long from the early morning sunshine and smoke glass coming out of my mouth so unusual for it to still be cold in the desert now in February.

I walk up under the porch and shadowed, stand there, the front-door handle is broken. This is the point. I look at the handle again. And there is only desert behind me and the sound of gravel under a car and the absent smell of earth.

I open the door—"Case, I came in because I heard Gaudi barking in the bathroom and you should really try and remember to take her out after you put her in there and you look like you need a drink"—and I'm in the house by now and it's cool in here, too, and the dog I got sometime a few weeks ago from somewhere I don't remember is wagging her tail at me and rubbing her head against mine and I absent-mindedly pet her and my neighbor extends a drink and says it looks like I need one and it's the last thing I want and so I say yes.

I drink it and it burns and I prayer my head and I blink the heavy sheet metal off my eyelids. The paw and the lonely barks nudge slowly at the pain and peel away the tissue wallpaper there on the place where my heart should be, one strip at a time. My sobs inaudible, hardly breathing, like underwater, and the voice in my ribs starts saying, *Just a little oxygen. Just a little, Case. Just enough to keep us going Case, just enough to keep us breathing, just enough to keep the snow so the dark doesn't swallow*, and I glimmer. Our lord and savior. Head bowed and drink my way back to home again.

Every afternoon by the end of the gold, after lying on the couch, trying not to sob, I slowly get up and know, both hands in my lap, that it's going to happen again tonight. And I'll make that phone call and they'll come—"Eight baskets, please. And a couple of forties." Somewhere in there the language for the pulse that is my lord, the medicine for my broken insides. And we'll start drinking, sometimes at Jake's, hardly ever at mine—"Get the junkie out of here"—and I leave.

Special.

The guys come in and I put Gaudi in the bathroom again and she hates them. Sometimes in there for days, I forget her, my black-and-white puppy.

Gene always showed up in a white truck. White fitted *ughn.* "Sit down. Gentlemen, hello." I'm walking through mud when I let them in, still strung out from earlier, and we sit on the couch, the one I found down the street, and it has flowers on it like wallpaper. I look at it, and then Gene's chest is crawling with drawing god dark cholo tattoos under open shirts and wife beaters, gold chains: "John, this is Casey, Casey this is my brother, John." Like the Bible and I know they are not blood. "Please, sit down," and they do on the flowers. John hands me some weed from the wide coat he's kept on and I reach across the shadow blur that is this living room and look at it, juicy. "Everybody wants something to come down"—like the time I smoked and sat under a palm tree and thought that I should do this all the time because the sun was like honey and my heart beat slowly and my lips smacked. "I can get those kids up in the foothills, they're white like me—you're not," I say, pointing at them with one hand cigarette: and they leave me with 5 lbs. of weed, 2 lbs. of coke, and 100 hits of acid. I shake their tattooed arms and shadow baggy pants, gold chains, and we stand in my living room. The empty house echoes differently with the weight of the shelves and I put the dreamers in the freezer, small squares I won't ever use because my mind is too fucked up with dark demons for hallucinogens that will keep me and never let me come back, and I put the weed and the coke like a book on the bookshelf the way I learned to in Atlanta. Through the kitchen window, I see Gene's truck drive away.

His thing is pills: white little vessels. A girl named Lauralene is addicted to them too. Her fingernails are perfect and she always smells clean like porn and her tits make her back hurt they are so tight and heavy behind her t-shirts and she says she takes pills because of them. She sucks Gene's dick for some if I'm not holding—sometimes I wish I was holding just to see her beg. I have her panties on the antenna of the U-Haul truck I ride around in for a few weeks after driving it to LA to help Dan move and deliver cocaine—he's not a friend, just a broken Swedish diver (like I'm a swimmer) going to LA for dreams. This time it will be better; no friends, except maybe my sister Sue this spring break, otherwise jerks who match my insides and I don't care, their dirt like the crud in my brain looking out from the doorway we all stare out from waiting for the next one to come.

And Sue is here on spring break, too, with her boyfriend Adam, and we go by sweet Brian's house before we leave for LA and I bring cocaine and pot, and even though I've quit swimming, they're still on the team healthy with ginseng drinks, and I give them some like they've ordered, no big deal, whatever habit now, since they know I can and do, I pet the big Akita dogs that live there and they lick my open palm. While Sue and Adam are outside drinking beer with Afrikaaner Erik and his roommates, Brian and I make out under his fan that whirls above me round and round and round, with his girlfriend's black lace panties twirling up there on the blade. Everything is silent but for the hum of the blades. Brian never tried to sleep with me, but only once this time putting my cunt in his face and then never again. My cunt coughed and made sounds while he was in there and I was pretending to feel something, and I try not to think that it's because I'm gross but that because he loves me, and he pats my head and holds me instead. This means something, I think.

Sue, Adam, Dan, and I leave Brian's house at sunset for Cali and slide in close behind semis the whole way, riding on their wind tails carrying us so we don't have to put our pedal foot on the gas, like a daredevil skill acquired to fly. We scurry around in the desert for sixteen hours, like beetles from god's eye view, because we drive around in a circle when we see the California border after four hours and try to look for another way around but we pass by it twice so we give up. The border police stop us anyway. As they mirror under the truck, my brain hardly lands near the vials in the glove compartment and under the seat, not thinking more than that it's mine, not theirs: they are wholly oblivious to what we're actually doing, heads hanging loose and the whites of our eyes hang out the window as we drive away greeting the rising moon dead over the scales of the trees. The cops find nothing.

Tinsel streams over LA when we get there, the buildings are like fireflies rising from concrete and we unpack the U-Haul into a stranger's house and I know that Dan is hustling him with his butt out where the stranger, standing in the window, can see him. I record him while he does it on my video camera image maker, dancing for a faggot. The light is perfectly dusk blue and my sister has glitter in her eyes tucked into the armchair and across the way are lines and lines from the buildings next door and we take more.

She's with me at the gay club that night where we are lovers because I need her to be where that boy over there shaking his head bent over the speaker asking for ass and I make her put her hand in mine like my girlfriend—"So they like us," I tell her, and "So they trust us so I can sell to them."

Into the apartment of darkness these big guys come dressed in all black button-ups and fitteds and I stand up because I called them and for the first time they are strangers and this is not Tucson and there are five more of them behind him and I feel small and an amber vial gets given to whoosh the black hole and they make me pay for it without even letting me taste it and I've never seen anything so fucking small like *Is this the size of your fucking dick?* I lean toward them and Sue pulls my arm and the other guys behind the asshole move their hands under their shirts, just to the sides of their hips, and I say "Fuck you" and throw them the money and the vials get tossed on the counter between me and them and they leave.

Then up the hills to the Hollywood sign in the early morning and everyone is running or jogging and Sue and I still have our heels on and we feel magical and beer bottles in our backpacks clank the glacier that is the mind strung across days of sleeplessness. "Are you on a fashion shoot?" someone asks and makes me feel special, and the glamorous. And then home where they still think we're lovers so they tuck us into the same bed even though there isn't anyone left in the bedroom to convince.

I do not get in the water when we find a jacuzzi on our way back to tucson.

My heart thumps loud, then slows, and I know this is bad. I do not tell them under the setting sun in a different desert that Communion in a water bath makes my heart attack and

I may die but do not want to so I don't get in and pretend it's because I am cold but it's because I can't tell them I've done too much and am lonely floating here in the sky with the loud noise. And they sit there and the sun sets blue again and then orange. That was the beginning a few days ago in LA and I can't tell if I'm here now.

Sue and I went home to Tuscon that morning or the morning after and we weren't sure where Dan was because we had ridden on a dragon on a Hollywood sign that day and we got back somehow not even remembering the trip home to Tucson, with just Adam this time, having left Dan in LA in the dark corner of a nightclub.

Swinging by the gas station afterward back in Tucson, I am filthy, and the guys in grease whites at the station, pointing to the truck's antenna, ask me if those are my panties and if I'm a dancer and then the nights start and The Black Sheep where the girl strippers walk like empty seashells with eyeliner and I am the snow dripper, fly pussycat, fly. Into the bar where we land mid-afternoon back in Tucson and I think, *This can't be right: Why am I drinking beer at 3?* and I've dropped Sue off at the airport and had a fix, for the first time in the airport parking lot, because her leaving was the wind sucked out of my chest without breathing. I snort my assured plunge into the abyss of hell for it. I forced her to act like my lover and gave her snow and brought her here for spring break. Spring break. I look ahead of me head up and my hands grip the steering wheel; now I am fine bright metal white sun on the dashboard again. And when the brothers from the Bible come back over to the house that night I tell them coke is shit expensive in LA and we should break into the fags over there. So we decide yes.

You don't have to live like this anymore.

It's a voice loud like god and I'm curled up on the rooftop and we're playing hide-and-go-seek under a full moon and Sue's been gone since a few days ago and I see night shadows wander sideways below me like ants. I've eaten a pizza under the streetlight glowing neon in the car, thinking that it would make my heart go normal—I don't even know where I am right now—and it hasn't. I see a kid dash by in the dark and I look. I wander around the squares that are these houses with wooden fences around them and find a drainpipe and climb it to the sky and sit on the roof and watch the ants wander below because they can't find me and then the hand of god speaks: *You don't have to live like this anymore,* says the moon sky and the streetlight glowing god and my black cloak over my shoulders like a shadow is the hiding cape.

"Hey, Uncle Bruce, I think I have a problem," I say into the phone the day or week before I have to buy a gun. When

I came back from LA someone had tried to break into my house again—the doorknob wobbly and the door itself bent inwards where something big had pushed against it. I need a gun and this is my normal somehow and I also can't figure out why that is. So I call my dad's brother, Uncle Bruce— Uncle Bruce in Boulder City—where the desert grew my father up, and Gaudi was next door at my neighbor's—had I asked him to watch her? Every time I walked over there to get her I'd walk behind his parents' house to the shed he lived in and he would open the door and the cave be- hind him would look black and dim red and three dogs would slowly walk out like panthers and I wondered if he fucked them because there was only enough room in there for the shade of his small mattress on the floor. I would walk Gaudi's paws back to my house and be a good parent to her for an hour until I had to fix myself with the blow or until Gene and his white truck came over. One night I came home and she had eaten my glasses and had also eaten a quarter pound bag of mushrooms I'd left on the couch. Hallucinogens not my thing, I wasn't mad that they'd gone to the hound, but I did have people over for the next few days to smoke cigarettes and watch this dog I now had that wouldn't move from the corner of the living room—she was tucked away there, tripping her doggy balls off, I guess, until I don't remember when she came out of the corner, but she eventually did.

And isca has sex with me.

When I go visit him that December in Seattle because he's good and he's left the woman with dark curly hair who sang and sucked his dick with a small waist when I didn't and couldn't but now, and I drink all his wine and don't understand why he only buys the smallest bottle of vodka at the grocery store but I pretend that I do and he jerks off in the shower after he doesn't come inside me and asks me if I want to watch but I say no and pass out under Seattle gray, looking through his bedroom window that's like the one we first had when we met in the desert. In the silence here with the shower muffled down the hallway here in this house where maybe I could live and be his wife and he'll save me, I can't tell if he loves me. I want him to. My eyes blink once and he drinks a fresh juice in the morning and I'm afraid it will kill me so I put vodka in it, clear, clean, to make it safe, glass is good and I know I can't stay here with orange juice.

Isca visits me in Tucson once after that and has sex with me that night. I'm not sure we spoke, and when we wake up, he says I'm the weirdest person he's ever had sex with and I roll away from him the next morning on the mattress on my floor where it's bright in the desert now without curtains and hurts my skin so I hide it, and "Oh, you've never had sex with someone who's blacked out?" and only remember him fucking me from behind fetal position being rocked back and forth while my head wobbled soft against my pillows thinking this is a lullaby—*casey casey bo-bacey banana-nana fo facey, cay-sey*—and that's some sort of kid's rhyme: Who taught me that? And when he comes to visit the next day to say good-bye, we sit outside my empty house under the porch awning and it's afternoon and we're in the shade, squatting down on the ledge in front of my front door, and the sun is white white white out there so our eyes squint and I tell him people are trying to break into my house so I'm buying a gun and he asks me what happened to me from when we first met, looking at me from behind his sunglasses so I can't see his eyes as tears stream down from behind them, making dust marks from the desert on his cheeks. I ignore them and I see them and I don't know why he didn't tell me he loved me years ago when I loved him and was still good and I'm not sure either. I say none of this. And I turn away from him and tell him again that I need to buy a gun and I look out to the sun and it blinds me when he leaves.

I need to buy a gun and isca looks at me.

Curled up in the corner—my old sweet friend, Brian. "Brian, I think something bad is happening." I called him after coming home—I had been dropped off and the driver-friend person who I had been spending time with said, "Case, you don't look so good. Are you sure you don't need help?" Meow meow, that's what the strippers were saying that night.

One of the Shes, Mandy, was doing her laundry and her thong stuck to her hips and outlined a perfect V to her low-rider jeans and she bent over and loaded up her laundry in Eric's kitchen. There's another one like a poster across from me—I think your name is Lesley—framed I can't see you or hear you, really, but the table is there and we are sitting at it and I can feel it under my hands and you are saying meow and your hair is like a whirlwind of perfect brown curls and your face is long like elegance and your eyes are so lost and I'm not sure why it is that we are both here, you seem so kind. Head down, curls falling on your eyes, you're meowing, telling us a story about a cat. White tank top and Mandy bending over to the right of my eyeball, leaning against the washer, telling us about her kid. That kid. Which kid. Who has a kid? My head slowly moves to look at her but the thought moves faster and with Mandy in my eye frame I've already moved back to the meow—to you—but Mandy's not what I'm looking at anymore even though I can hear her—you are—and Mandy's words are coming out of your mouth. Your voice has changed.

And it's black dark outside and the overhead light from the '80s flying saucer is making everyone look yellow and tepid green. And I'm in the yard and Daniella comes up to me, short dumpy hair and grease everywhere from being human, and asks me, "Hey, you got some?" and I say, "Yeah," and then someone later that night tells me that Daniella is never anyone you want to tell you're holding because she'll stalk you and hunt you down and fuck you to score so I wonder if she'll sleep with me. And the morning air turns light blue again and my body is grated metal so that I have to move slowly and everyone talks about going ice-skating in the sky. "Can you drive me home?" And he does.

crawl on the floor is that fuzz there Technicolor? God. Please don't let me die today.

God

Crawl

and then I know I'm going to die so I grab my camera:

doorknob. click.

Our father who art in heaven hallowed be thy name. click.

Carpet. click. Mirror. click.

Our kingdom come thy will be done click

Reflection click

On earth as it is god. click.

Floor.

And then I call Brian and tell him I think something terrible is happening and I hear, "Why are you up so early? I have to go to swim practice," through the crackle receiver and he swings by on his way and I hear him coming through the door and if I don't die this time I'll never do this again, god, please don't let me die, and the last thing I see is Brian walking in and crouching horror to his sobbing face as his legs fall him to the corner of my bedroom because he doesn't know what to do. And that's how I die—with the gold morning light streaming in my window, my mattress on the floor, and I am in it, and Brian, tall strong brilliant man, fallen like Icarus to the edge of the two walls of my room, covering his face because death is lying there, and it's peaceful and I can't hear him anymore and everything is like staring straight into the sun.

"What are you doing?" I wake up my eyeballs and tuck my chin without moving my head, looking down at Jake's head on my chest. I push him off. "What the fuck?" And I've got a blue cool rag on my forehead and I throw it off and he looks at me, "I was just making sure your heart was still beating: it stopped last night and we put you in cold water and it started up again," and his tight unbuttoned polyester shirt is too close to me, his cold fingers petting my forehead. And I don't care and pass out—this time surely to sleep.

I wake up alone in my bedroom and I'm not sure what time it is and have the heavy in my chest weighing and I get up off the floor and see a blue rag by my bed and remember Brian curled in the corner but he's gone and walk out to my living room and see Jake and Mel fucking on my couch, slow coming down fucking with head rolled back and Mel's eyes are in the back of her head and she's blacked out I know and Jake is sort of grunting and stops when he sees me and leans off of her and Mel's eyes come back to her face and she stares at me and he does, too, and I walk to the kitchen and it seems like it's 5 o'clock afternoon gold outside but it's hard to say and how long have we been here, was this yesterday or are we today and tomorrow, how long did I sleep for and little white pills on the stove, hello, little Ecstasy cut with dope, and I pop one in my mouth and think I want two, and then walk back to the living room with a glass of water in my hand just having taken the first one and Jake looks at me and asks me what it is I just took and I say, "E," and Mel says, "Case, it's not even been ten hours," and I say, "Look. Look here." And I'm staring at them. And I drink my water and swallow heaven again. And sit on the chair across from them and there are plants I just bought though I'm not sure where I got the money from, and the bay window out to the driveway is lit up white from the afternoon sun and my last roommate moved out so I live here alone now and Mel and Jake untangle and Mel goes to the fridge and gets her jug of vodka out and sits next to Jake and he drinks some and no one says anything. Quiet gold day because there isn't much going on and it's spring break and we're up and slow this morning and the sky is already wide.

Prelude

Somewhere in between two weeks of sometime after that overdose and after my call to him uncle bruce buys me a ticket out of tucson.

All I can do is get high once I know I'm leaving. When I get on the plane that night, an airline stewardess leans in with her lipstick face and asks me if they need to turn the plane around on the tarmac. I look up at her with my head cricking off my body and hear my heart thump full of cocaine and know I'll die if I get off the plane. I have a bag of fifty needles at my house and Brie lined up to score and she ODs all the time. So I look at the airline stewardess and tell her I'm all right but to keep an eye on me, I have a heart condition and pat my heart and it falls into the seat behind me and goes away and my head rolls off my shoulders and I foam at the mouth and swallow dry before she sees it and she gives me a drink and I fall awake watching Tucson string up fairy lights, nighttime flying away from me to black in the sky so sad that I'll never see my friends again and my eyeballs are dry they crack and I miss them already. When I land in Vegas, Uncle Bruce is there and has tears in his eyes and he wipes them away with the back of his hand, the other holding mine, and I do not understand why, so I lean my head against his car window when I get in and feel how hard and cold it is there. I am coming down. Coming down. I am concrete and the wheels roll on through the window on my forehead.

After Uncle Bruce empties my house in Tucson a few weeks later, he gets back to Vegas and tells me he's never seen so many drugs in one house in his life—and he's from *Easy Rider*—I'm impressed and feel pleased. I don't remember how much I had except for the Vicodin Brie stole. I want it back. He brings Gaudi with him when he comes home and tells me some weird scrawny neighbor junkie was taking care of her next door and she and I walk the desert and I scream from there but the sand swallows the sound to nothing and Gaudi sniffs a bush and comes when I call her so I pet her. When Uncle Bruce calls my mom to tell her I'm not in Tucson anymore, she says on the phone crackling from France, *"Casey's always been a little dramatic, are you sure there's a problem?"* And Uncle Bruce hangs up the phone and looks at me from his La-Z-Boy and is sad in his eyes for me and shrugs his shoulders. That night we get drunk together and he leans into me, sitting on the white carpet floor in his living room, and says through his mustache, "Damn, I wish you weren't my niece," and pats my soft knee skin, and I don't know how to move. And that night in a silk nightie I wear I realize I need a robe if I'm going to stay here when I hear him slink away from my bedroom doorway. Here I masturbate to Jesus, lord our savior on the cross who is good to me and I think Uncle Bruce hears me come from my side room and starts listening for it. So I stop.

I've stopped shaking. The shaking has stopped. I want to go back to Tucson.

I stopped kicking only just a few days ago and I remember Aunt Lou walking out of the house for dinner last night in a silver dress that has silver sliver fringes all around it that splay out when Uncle Bruce twirls her when they dance and she is beautiful in her shiny pink lip gloss. I stay in and drink some more wine with Sprite like a seltzer: it cools my insides. We've bought bigger bottles of wine and I'm not sure why. I read *Snow Falling on Cedars* and then curl up oh the couch and watch *Leave It to Beaver* and think of my dad who grew up here in the 1950s under Sinatra and where his brother killed himself falling out of a plane coming back from Vietnam, like I learned suicide when I was twelve. I am here now and the desert is still the same at the edge of his house.

I call a rehab. I call them after coming to from eating the tissue out of the garbage that still has blow in it from being stuck in there from detoxing a few days ago. I let it dissolve in my mouth and hope it will give me the numb—and it doesn't and I swallow it.

"Okay, Casey, so you haven't had a drug in over two weeks but are you drinking?"

"Yeah."

"Okay, well, if you can, try to not drink again until you get here."

"Why would I do that?"

"Just try if you can. If you can't, don't worry about it— we'll see you when you get here."

The phone goes click when I look at it back in its place. Drinking? What the fuck.

Uncle Bruce and Aunt Lou drive me to the rehab center the next day, through the red desert to Utah, the rocks stand still and tall, watching us drive by them, small, in a car that glistens under the white sun. I do not know what is happening.

In rehab I do jumping jacks in the bathroom of my intake so my heartbeat is higher—they give me little pills that melt the glass shards in my gut and make me go smooth and quiet. I walk into my bedroom from the bright sun and into the shadows where a She's detoxing. My new roommate asks my why I'm here—I tell her without thinking: "I don't want to die." I'm surprised I say this: Why the fuck am I talking to her? Who the fuck is she? When I wake up from the night, I meet Lea. She's in here on a plea bargain for ten counts of attempted murder. She and her boyfriend got pulled over: ten

sawed-off shotguns in the back of his truck. He's in jail—
she's in here as an Accessory: I know her kind, they're the
dancers and the strippers to the guys, hookers like pussycats
fucking grime saying meow, meow, meow, so I let her sit next
to me anyway and she lets me touch the inside of her thigh
even though she doesn't want me to and I love her. Her hair
is stringy, greasy blond and she smells even though we're all
clean. She still has her rigs rolled up in her socks and that afternoon shoots up the dregs one last time and her eyes roll to
the back of her head and I watch her. She didn't have enough
for me and the next day I meet her two kids who come to
visit her with their grandmother and I feel weird because of
it: something isn't right—they are blond-haired, sweet tod-
dler Rex shows up as a patient a few days after me and I love
him. His smiley beard and sparkly eyes cooked meth up in
Mormon country where it's all coming from and they ride the
dragon real hard, trailer trash up there, and I love him and
I hear you're still the one I run to, the one that I belong to,
and my insides hurt I want his hands on me to hold me and
make me safe and love me and we dream of skipping out of
here with Max, who's under eighteen and steals mail trucks,
and we'll hot-wire a trailer from next door to drive up to Salt
Lake to sell meth and not use. We'll do that. Sell meth and
not use. I'll be his wife and he'll love me in my jean shorts
and dirty tank top and flip-flops, I'm the one. The cafeteria
ladies tell me they see the light in me and I don't eat the food
they serve me because I'm skinny now and I watch the sun

shine outside and the steeple from the temple sparkles on the horizon and they make me go change out of my skirt because it's too short and I think: *What?*

What am I doing here?

Where am I?

and the desert doesn't answer and for days after they stop giving me pills everything has edges on it that look like silver blades and it hurts walking through the air on my skin and my head slowly comes up from in the deep crevices it fell into. The desert says nothing and the sky blasts the colors of setting and I see it for the first time again.

April 23, 1998.

Yesterday I drank the alcohol the big security guard snuck in for us and then I hatched a plan to move up to Salt Lake and cook and I told Lea and Max this, perched up on my bed, my teeth grinding crazy, I looked at them in the dark—I have night vision. I've locked us in our room and they're looking at me like I'm nuts but they're the crazy ones and then the staff follows me into the swimming pool where I exercise the next day, that's today, and they frisk my towel and find a beer can in the locker trash can where I had tried to throw it away and they frisk my room then and find the rest and walk me back to the rehab without letting me get into the pool. Everyone else is quarantined away into the cafeteria.

Where are my friends? Where is *Saturday Night Fever* Jake? I miss him. I love him. "You have five minutes to pack your bags and leave." I stare at them. What about Rex and selling meth and you're still the one? "You have five minutes to pack your bags and leave."

"I'm sorry, what?"

"You broke the rules."

Wait. What is happening?

When they kick me out, they won't let me sit on the front lawn of the property. I scream at them "DON'T YOU KNOW WHO I AM? DON'T I EVEN GET A PHONE CALL?" and they do and I don't. And I'm scared and don't cry. I walk to the grassy edge of a storm drain and I promise myself that if I live I'll go skydiving. I fold up the paper I've written that on and put it away. The sun makes my eyes blink, so I do and see nothing but white. I turn twenty-one in three days. I know I'm going to die.

God.

The grass pokes at my flesh thighs, green and pointy; it scratches, and waiting under the midday scorching sun, breathing in the heat, I make a list.

That day I lose the last thing I have—that bed, in that rehab.

I have a small plastic bag with me. The skirts I have in it are short and folded up.

I look at the pile and sigh away from it, staring straight ahead of me.

I'm not wearing panties.

The guy who picks me up knew my dad. Apparently. And he'd left Vegas a year ago or so to get clean. I didn't remember his name when he drove up and he didn't ask me to. I just remember him telling me one day in rehab when he was visiting someone else that getting clean just wasn't gonna be as good as getting high. His number had somehow made it into my hand. So I called it from a pay phone down the street and the receiver burned my ear from being so hot standing like that in the phone booth outside in the desert with nothing around but empty and no sound.

I remember the last of the grass, parched, brittle, and dry, breaking underneath my feet as I walked across it barefoot to the car when he pulled up to drive me halfway back to Vegas. I heard the car door shut loud after I got in. I said, "Hey." "*Hey,*" he said, not looking at me. I put my seat belt on and it clicked. He had both hands on the wheel and they stayed there.

Uncle Bruce was waiting for us in the middle of the desert on the side of the road. Everything was so flat and dry, we could see his car and where we were meeting him from far away. This was the end of the world, with red dust watching us, and it took us another thirty minutes to get to him. The sky opened above me and I leaned in toward the dashboard as we got closer and I watched it through the windshield.

We pulled up and got out. There wasn't anything or anyone else for miles. Somewhere in between Utah and Nevada, the sky and the road stretched out and Uncle Bruce and the dude shook hands and hugged without a word. I got in Uncle Bruce's car and looked straight ahead at nothing, clicking the door closed behind me. The seat burned the back of my thighs while I waited for Uncle Bruce and the sky screamed white midday desert sun on me through the windshield like it used to in Tucson and I felt nothing and heard nothing and I bowed my head alone in there and I heard a faraway rumble and the sound of the spirit of god slowly moved out from the void and the darkness of the deep shifted out from the waters of the Atlantic, and across the oceans, over the plains and this desert, it rose until the Wide Hand of God said: Let there be light now on this creature; Let there be light—

and I did not lift my head

—*and there was.*

Acknowledgments

For my wife, Ms. Siri May. Thank you for sharing your searing mind, your brilliant heart, and your generous and fierce soul with me.

For Kraka and for Gaudi.

Thank you to my brother and my sisters for letting me tell this story.

This is how I remember it.

& I love you.

Thank you, Eric Dean Wilson, for your friendship and company, and your tirelessly keen eyes and ears in all the iterations that has been this godspeed.

ACKNOWLEDGMENTS

Thank you to my friend and agent Bill Clegg and my publisher, Peter Borland, who have tirelessly and with great humor tried to herd the writer in me who has her middle finger up to the world all the time—I feel like we succeeded.

About the Author

Casey Legler is an artist, restaurateur, model, and former Olympic swimmer. Born in France to expatriate American parents, Casey grew up in Provence, and went on to swim for France in the 1996 Summer Olympics in Atlanta. The first woman signed to Ford Models to exclusively model men's clothes, Casey has been featured in *Vogue*, *Le Monde*, and *Time*. She is a member of Phi Beta Kappa, graduated cum laude from Smith College, and currently divides her time between New York and Sydney, Australia, with her wife, Siri May.